Our Little Ones

A Few Games for Parents, *or*, A Delightful Upbringing

Stephanie L. Mckay

Copyright © 2012 Stephanie K. Mckay. All rights reserved.
ISBN 978-0-9917416-5-6

Our Little Ones

A Few Games for Parents, *or*, A Delightful Upbringing

Children are the flowers of life. It's up to a man to give a woman as many of these flowers as he can. And it's up to a woman to accept this gift and carry it throughout of her entire life. The sad thing is that fewer and fewer women today are prepared to accept such a gift. And even if they are prepared to do so, then they aren't always able to find someone from whom they'd like to receive such a bouquet.

Where do children come from? Are they a gift from above, or can we plan them? Why do childless couples exist? How do families with many children come about? What is the secret of how children come into the world? And once they've come into the world, how can we make them happy? In this book, I give some partial answers to these questions. But my main goal in this book is not to entertain you with a series of theories about how children arrive in the world. Rather, I would like readers to reflect on their relationships with the opposite sex, on their relationships with their children, and think about how important it is to live out this life in harmony with those close to them, above all, with their children. To think about how to bring them up properly, so that life will be joyful for everyone.

This book is a textbook of sorts, one that can help you build harmonious relationships with your children. I've written it bearing in mind both current psychological theories on raising children, as well as my own personal child-rearing experience. This book will be of interest not only to parents who are raising children in intact families, but also to moms and dads raising their children on their own.

From the Author

What prompted me to write a book about raising children? The first reason is my own upbringing, in other words, the childhood upbringing I myself received from my parents. I refer to these memories as "tales of a guinea pig," because that's exactly what I was during the years I was growing up. The second reason is the experience I gained raising my own children. I gained the bulk of this experience through my relationship with my older son, which was rather complicated for reasons beyond both our control. Several factors came together here: our complete astrological incompatibility, the fact that both of us like to be in charge, my lack of experience in raising children, plus the fact that he was approaching adolescence, a period that's terrifying to enter. I was also motivated to write the book by my interest in psychology. Like any science, child psychology has become overgrown with a thick layer of theoretical knowledge, but it also suffers from a deficit of practical applicability. Psychologists have come up with a great variety of tests designed to help us know our children better, methods for developing this or that quality in them, but for one reason or another, the majority of these can't help us enrich our everyday contact with our children. Most of these works are theoretical in nature and don't offer parents any significant practical aid. Of course, these works are worthy of our attention, and I'll talk about them below. But in my book I'd like to pay more attention to the practical aspect of child rearing, to simple but indispensible tips that help us build our relationships with our children on a daily basis. And help us build not just the parent-child relationship itself, but harmonious, trusting, loving interactions in general.

The book contains an appendix with some games we came up with in our family to make the long winter nights go faster. These games are suitable for the whole family. I've tested them on my own children, and they have a wonderful way of bringing the entire family together and putting everyone in the family in a good mood. I've also included several interesting tests developed by practicing psychologists, tests that will help you determine one's dominant character traits. They can help parents get their bearings in this job of raising children, a job that is both so complex and of such great consequence.

Honesty

**To be fair and honest with our children without hiding from them
what is going on in our souls – that is the sole way to educate them**
   L. Tolstoy

It goes without saying that raising and educating a child is an interesting and multi-faceted process. But I feel that educating a child means first and foremost educating oneself. I don't consider child-rearing some separate process you have to learn or worry yourself about or which you have to approach with intent focus. Certainly, professional educators and child care professionals who work with others' children really do need to take an interest in this – they need to familiarize themselves with new educational methods, read in their field and keep their qualifications up to date. Simply because of the nature of their profession, they work with children who have already been affected to some extent by their parents. These professionals are faced with the task of re-educating children, which is a much more complex business. As for the parents, they have ready access to an assistant that's better than any of the most advanced methods: parental love. True, this love can hurt as much as it helps, if the parents' love is so blind as to trump their good sense. I address this topic in more detail in the chapter "Blind Love." In such cases, though, it's the parents who need educating, not the children. For this reason, in most cases, the children are just like their parents or, to put it a different way, they carry within them everything that's in their parents. There's even a saying along these lines: "the apple doesn't fall far from the tree. " What can a mom and dad instill in their child? Only what they themselves possess. What's more, it's been noted that parents' traits always manifest themselves much more prominently in their children. For example, a given negative trait in a mother's character will be more prevalent in the daughter than in the mother. The same is true of positive character traits. For example, if a father is generous, then the son can end up being generous to a fault. It's also true that the parents' life scripts repeat themselves in the children. They can do so in a worse way than in the parents' lives, or, conversely, in a better way, but in general the children will follow the same course as the parents. The American psychologist Eric Berne wrote extensively and in detail about the life paths of children and parents. The upshot is that the first thing you need to do is change yourself, even though achieving this in practice, in real life, is a much more complicated matter. We can tell ourselves a hundred times that we'll start living some new way, but then, the 101st time, we'll do exactly what we've done our whole lives. Again, if we're fated to radically change, it will just happen. Our own personal efforts will play absolutely no role in it. Sure, when change does happen, we can pound our chests and say, "I changed," or "I've gotten kinder," and so on. But the only things that happen in life are those that are supposed to happen. So, in general I think it's better to downplay the role that any sort of personal authorship plays, whether in your own destiny or your child's. Given that this is the case, my views on childrearing boil down to simply spending a child's childhood with him.

When I'd just begun writing this book, my ten-year old son asked what my book was about. I told him it was about raising and educating children. He shrugged and said, "Why write about that? No matter what you do, children will grow up to be the way they are. Educate me or don't – either way I'll be the way I am." I decided to continue discussing this topic and added, "You know, I'm basing this book based on my experience raising my own children, and I don't want you to grow up with, say, the same traits I'm encouraging my readers to conquer in themselves. After all, what kind of educator am I if I haven't managed to bring up my own children properly?" My son answered, "If I grow up different than the way you'd like me to be, what do you have to do with it? I'm the one who'll grow up. You're the one who feels the raising is necessary – it makes you feel calmer. You think you're raising us, but really you're not raising us at all." "How can that be?" I protested. "What do you mean I'm not raising you? Sometimes I even punish you." "No, you just write your books, and you punish us when you get mad." That's how our conversation happened. I've copied it down here word for word. Yes, sometimes children are smarter than their parents.

On the one hand, I was very pleased by this discussion with my son. As one classicist said, if you devote yourself entirely to raising your children, you can be sure they'll hate you! That means my approach to childrearing is still within reasonable limits, since my children don't even notice it. At least I don't have to worry that they'll hate me. But on the other hand, it turns out there's nothing in particular to write about. If all there is to raising children is to simply live out their childhood alongside them – and that is exactly how I see it – then why waste any words? I am firmly convinced that children are the reflection of our inner essence. That is, whatever way we are inside is how our children will be, too. But if we don't have the strength to change ourselves – and we *don't* have the strength to do this – then why torment our children by demanding *they* be a certain way? And so, in that case, what can one write in a book about raising children? Should one prod parents to change themselves for the better, so their children will change, too? It's a noble prodding, to be sure, but what's good will it do? We say we'd be happy to change, but that's nothing more than words. If we're easily irritated and shout at our child at the drop of a hat, then we'll continue on in that same vein, even if all the books in the world urge us to do the opposite. You can urge people to show a child only their best qualities, so that he'll copy the best of what's in us. But what should you do with the bad qualities? After all, you can't mask them. There are negative sides of any person's character. So, it seemed to me that the more correct approach is to urge parents to act naturally – with their children, at least. We so often play various roles in our life – at work, with our friends, with our relatives. We've even started playing roles with our children – the role of a father or a mom, the role of a strict mother or a better father. We behave unnaturally with our children so often. And all because we're trying to be better than we really are. We don masks and sometimes get so caught up in the play that we forget to remove the masks even when we're with our children. Many psychologists even urge us to play games like these with our children, urge us to control our emotions when we interact with our children. For example, the author of one book tells mothers never to cry in the presence of their children. And he justifies his suggestion by saying that only happy mothers can have happy children. It's a snazzy justification, and I totally agree with it. But who better for a child to learn from, if not from his mother, that life has not only a bright side, but a dark side as well? That far from everything is under our control, that life brings not only joy, but sadness as well, not only smiles, but tears, too. Who better than a mother to serve as an example for her child about how to make your way through life's unpleasant situations? Who better than a mother to teach her child about compassion and caring about others? And who will a child will care about more than anyone on earth, if not his mother? Through feeling sorry for his mother, a child learns to feel sorry for others. For this reason, if one can express in words what "upbringing" means, then the most correct word would probably be honesty. An upbringing carried out with honesty is the best kind there could be in a family. If we don't hide what is going on in our soul, we'll be able to count on the same honesty and openness on the part of our children. That's the only way open family relationships are possible. For this reason, I consider the actual process of educating and raising children to be the process of educating and raising myself. It's not a methodology and not a process of molding someone. It's simply our life with our child, our sincere interaction with him.

It's true that we can interpret "honesty" in two ways. For example, in family therapy, the topic of honesty always elicits a great number of debates among couples who are going through a divorce. If a wife detests her husband in every way and considers him a traitor and a cheater, then she'll take the call for candor totally literally. She'll be prepared to pour out all the dirt on her husband to their child. Because that's also being honest. I categorically oppose honesty in a case like this, even if the child is grown and fully capable of grasping what has happened. Really, you can't pour out all the dirt on the father to the child. But then the mother wonders, "Why should I be deceptive and not share everything inside me with my children, not let them know everything that's going on? After all, I need to be open and honest." If the child hears something bad about his father from someone else, that could be very, very traumatic. But if he hears it from his mother, the trauma will last his whole life. First of all, his dad hurt his mom. Second, his dad ended up being a bad guy. How can a child wrap his mind around that? And the third reason honesty should be dispensed in small doses in such cases is that the person who hurt you is the father of your children. Really, if you found it possible to love him, to bear his children, then of course you'll find it possible to forgive him, too, even if your relationship can't return to what it was. So, at this point in time, why add insult and lack of forgiveness into the mix of your child's emotions? There's no way doing that can ease the pain, but it can definitely increase it.

Independence

"My child's three years old. At what age can we start educating him?"
"Madame, you're exactly three years too late."

Virginia Satir, one of my favorite American psychologists, once said, "I'm convinced that the way my daughter could hurt me most would be to come to Christmas dinner only because she was afraid I'd get offended if she didn't. It would show me that I'd failed to teach her to be independent."

By the way, independence is exactly what parents fear in their children. They fear it because when the child gains independence, the parents lose control over him. And when they lose control, they're afraid they'll produce an incompetent person or loser, someone who'll choose the wrong path and won't succeed in life. More than anything on earth, parents are afraid they'll end up with an offspring who's gotten out of hand. After all, they're convinced that he can't survive without them. They're convinced that they're capable of directing their child to the right path, of setting the right priorities for him, of inculcating the right thoughts in him, or in other words, of cultivating a worthy member of society. And all they need in order to achieve this is for the child to obey them. Because, after all, if he doesn't obey them, how can he achieve the best in life, all that his parents have prophesied for him? This is where one of the most important and dangerous illusions about upbringing arises – the idea that sure it's important to cultivate independence in a child, but that's not the most important thing. Parents are convinced that children need independence at a more mature age, at the point when the child has a clear understanding of what he wants from life and is capable of pursuing that goal steadfastly. That's certainly true, but where's he going to get that independence at a more mature age if it was squelched in childhood? We're so fond of interfering in our children's business, helping and protecting them, and we refer to this using the lovely phrase "caring about them." And because of all this we don't give our children any opportunity to act on their own. In reality, one of the simplest rules for developing independence is not to butt into what a child's doing if he doesn't ask for help. When parents use this approach, they're sending their child this message: "Of course you can do it! You'll do it!" And the second rule, the logical extension of the first, is not to leave a child to fend for himself when he really does need help. Doing that sends this message: "This doesn't matter, and you won't be able to do it."

I love watching children. It's particularly fun to watch naughty children. They fear no one and nothing. Punishment, their parents' strict shouting, the presence of outsiders – all of these mean nothing to them. They keep up the mischief and take great pleasure in it. Naughty children are always full of energy and joy. And it's nothing but a pleasure to observe them. But it's an even greater pleasure to observe the parents who are patient enough not to interrupt this sweet process of getting to know the surrounding world. After all, although to us this seems like misbehaving, for the child it's just a fun game. Giving permission to "be creative" opens the door to confidence for the child, and confidence in turn leads to self-sufficiency. Only a self-confident person is capable of making decisions, capable of taking action no matter what the circumstances, capable of displaying will and independence. Confidence gives rise to independence. But if a child is going to be confident, we need to offer him a "carrot." Confidence is perhaps the only personality trait that using the "stick" can't help develop. Only a system of incentives and encouragement will work here. Criticism, laughter, irony, denying permission, and a fear of giving a child responsibility are all enemies on the path to developing a child's confidence. It's very easy to inculcate low self-esteem in a child, and very difficult for him to free himself from it. It's nearly impossible for him to do so on his own. If one day you demean your child's qualities in some way, demean his achievements and efforts, it's not enough to just praise him the next time. The idea "I'm bad" gets stored away in the cellular memory much more deeply than any subsequent "I'm good" pattern. Your child is more likely to believe the "I'm bad" than the "I'm good." Certainly, an experienced psychologist will be able to help raise the child's self image, but it's far better not to lower it in the first place.

As you go about developing your child's confidence, don't be afraid to praise him, to delight in his smallest achievements, to let him do grown-up things. However, as far as praise is concerned, there really is such a thing as too much of a good thing. Sometimes you can go overboard. *You should have a reasonable basis and firm motivation for any praise*, any delight. Otherwise you'll get a child with an oversized sense of pride, which is just as hard to manage as low self-esteem. It's a double-edged sword. Your task is to take the middle way without slipping off either edge. It's not a simple task, just like the overall process of raising a child. Analyze one day of your interactions with your child. Try to count how many times you've responded to him with positive utterances (a joyful greeting, validation, encouragement) and how many times you've responded negatively (a reproach, a reprimand, criticism.) If the number of negative interactions is equal to or greater than the number of positive interactions, then it means your relations aren't productive.

In reality, raising a child is not as difficult or tedious as it might seem from reading a few books on child-rearing. Psychologists love to complicate things a bit and use scientific approaches where you need to use love. On a related note: it can seem that raising a child is something requiring specialized pedagogical knowledge and training. That's partly the case, and partly not. If there's not enough love, then various methods can help, and that's not a bad thing, either. But really, if you look just a little deeper, you'll see that child-rearing can become a very sweet and fun part of our lives. After all, raising our children gives us the chance to raise ourselves, too. We can grow, change and improve ourselves together.

What could be more wonderful than to raise a crop and then see the harvest come in? Of course, sometimes something goes wrong and there's a bad harvest: the parents aren't pleased with the fruits. They aspired to raise one kind of fruit, and they ended up with some thing different. Here's some food for thought: does this happen because the seeds are bad, because they haven't been tended correctly, or because the initial aspiration was wrong? I'll discuss this in detail in the chapters that follow.

Habits

"Daddy, guess which train is running the latest of all."
"Which one, sonny?"
"The one you promised to get me for Christmas last year."

Unfortunately, for many of us, childrearing turns into a process of eliminating our own faults in our children. And we engage in this elimination unconsciously. Or, more accurately, we don't see these faults in ourselves, but we see them quite clearly in our children. Even when we do see them, there's nothing we can do about them. But because we've long since lost any hope of fixing anything in ourselves, it seems to us that we can still fix something in our kids. Thus begins the great process of upbringing. We nag our children and order them to do something. For example, we tell them not to pick their nose, or tell them to pick up around the house, or take out the trash. And we call this the process of socializing them or getting them used to work, or something else. The child resists. And that's a very good thing, because that shows you haven't yet squelched his will and that he's still capable of putting up a fight. In the opposite case, when he no longer has any will, you're raising a biorobot with repressed resistance functions. I don't want the reader to take this as a call to dispense with ordering the child to do anything at all. There can be orders. But if you take a reasonable approach, then they aren't orders at all, but rather responsibilities, the same kind every person has, including a child. You can think of orders as something you can carry out or something you can also ignore. Responsibilities are more like something you have to do just because you have to do it. They're closer to necessities. For example, the child experiences the need to get dressed, to cover his body with clothing. This need doesn't arise because you've ordered the child to do this. Rather, it's because you yourself always do it, and so do other people. And the child will do it, too. So it turns into a necessity. In the same way, our vital responsibilities become necessities if there's a point to them. When you think about it, there's a point to the clothing you put on every day: it keeps you warm, it covers your nakedness, which we also do for a specific reason, and so on. The child begins to do this gradually, without you reminding or shouting at him, because it has to be done. He won't think to ask you about the reasons. Fostering a sense of responsibility is an element of upbringing. Fostering. Not shouting, not demanding, not punishing. All of these come into play if the sense of responsibility hasn't been fostered, if that moment has been lost. When that happens, that's when parents begin making up for lost time by trying various childrearing methods. Of course, none of them will work. And then we slap on a label on the child and say that he's a "difficult" child, out of control.

Everything would be so easy and simple if it were relatively easy to explain the point of every responsibility to a child. For example: you need to put your dirty socks in the laundry basket because the smell of sweat fills the room, and when you breathe that in, you're swallowing germs. You don't have to just explain this; you can also illustrate it using any methods you want, or by inviting your family doctor to come over and confirm the dangers of the smell of sweat. But I'll bet that the next day, after this talk, the socks will still be lying in the same place instead of in the laundry basket. Or, there's a second possibility: once he hears the talk, the child will start picking up the socks, but will then revert to his old habits. That's like an acquired habit. As we gain life's experience, a system of reflexive connections is established in our cerebral cortex. This system is called a dynamic stereotype. It lies at the root of many habits and skills. For this reason, if the habit of putting things where they go hasn't already been established in a child, then it won't be developed as quickly as the parents might like. And it's not the child's fault. That's the way our physiology is. There's a different cause. How did the child develop the habit of throwing everything everywhere? Because in the family it was never considered essential that everything be in its place. Whether that's good or bad isn't important. What's important is that we're wanting the child to do something we've never fostered in him and, what's more, something we've never done regularly ourselves. And that's where our problem lies. We strive to instill a desire for cleanliness in our child at the same time as we ourselves don't strive for it. For example, cleanliness among moms who are obsessed with hygiene generally becomes an integral feature of the household. The children in this house will take showers, put their things away and brush their teeth twice a day, all without any reminders. And it's not because they're clean freaks and other people are slobs. It's just that for them, stepping into the shower is just as much a reflexive necessity as it is for others to go to the bathroom. There's no secret method of upbringing at work here. It's nothing more than the imitation of adults, an imitation that in time grows into a daily necessity for the child. Or take one more example: the parents want the child to watch less television, in spite of the fact that they themselves love to spend their free time at home in front of the TV. So we ask, how should the child spend his free time? Of course, we want him to go to basketball camp or do karate instead of watching TV. But what good does it do him? You can lecture him on the benefits of sports, or of being able to stand up for yourself, or you can just sign him up for a camp, but that's not likely to work, and even if it does, it won't work for long. On a related note: before demanding that your child do something, it makes sense to take a look at yourself. You might actually be amazed at the similarities between your habits and your child's. You can explain this by saying it's genetics, or ordinary imitation. A child imitates everything, just like a little monkey. He'll adopt both the bad and the good. Now at this point, the attentive reader might ask how to explain the fact two children who have grown up in the same family can be absolutely different from each other. For example, two brothers might be entirely different, and two sisters might share no similarities. If the age difference between them is small and the children are of the same sex, then they can have entirely different personalities and not look at all alike, but then still develop the same habits that they've adopted from their parents. They'll have the very same habit of making their beds, putting away their clothing, cleaning up their toys, and so on. If the age difference is four or more years, then you might well see a bit of difference in their habits, because one of them is the older brother or sister, and the parents will often give him or her a task they feel the younger sibling can't do on his own. In such cases, the younger children might not develop the same habits as the older ones, despite growing up in the same family. It might even turn out, in such a situation, that the children are not at all like each other. In this case, the younger ones develop different habits. For example, they hand more task off to the other child than they take on themselves, or they procrastinate, or don't do things they've been asked to do on time (a very common habit among younger siblings,) etc. When this happens, it becomes obvious that it isn't that the child chooses his habits – whether to make his bed or not, whether to brush his teeth or not. Rather, these habits develop in him as he interacts with the people around him. If the child interacts only with his parents, then they'll be the sole indicators of the habits he'll adopt, because they're the ones he'll imitate. If there are several children in the family, then they'll all imitate each other as they interact. For example, you'll often hear a mom ask her daughter, "Have you ever seen my underwear strewn around the way yours is?" The daughter really might never have seen her mother's underwear strewn around, but she *has* seen her mother consistently leave all her other clothing lying around. The child won't get bogged down in details and figure out that you have to hide your underpants away, but you can leave your dress hanging on a chair because it's a dress. The child does everything by reflex. Who ever told her that underpants are bad and you have to hide them, but that dresses are good? Once she gets a little older, the girl may automatically start hiding her underwear in her dresser, but her other clothing will most likely stay strewn about.

Personality

**If you want to develop your character,
then you have to perform feats of heroism
at least twice a day. That's exactly what I do:
every morning I get up and every night I go to sleep.
- William Somerset Maugham**

As our observations of children show, we don't have the power to affect our child's personality; we don't have the power to change it, to make it gentler or, at the opposite extreme, tougher. The personality is the way it is. If we're sometimes unable to change even ourselves – for example, by changing from being shy to being bold, or from taking things slow to running around in a frenzy, then how can we possibly change our children? Of course, we have the illusion that while the child is still little, then we can mold him into something, we can shape his personality and develop certain traits. But this is nothing more than an illusion. We don't mold a child into anything, any more than our parents molded us into anything. A child's personality takes shape the way it does as a result of many factors, none of which depends on us. You can say that we're given a personality and it's not within our power to change it. But it *is* within our power to minimize the expression of some sides of the personality, say, the negative sides, and to enhance the expression of others. And here's where the goal of upbringing lies. When a baby's a newborn, it seems that he doesn't have any personality as yet, that it will all take shape as he gets older. But that's one of the mistakes we make. He already has a personality. It's just that he's not showing it so clearly as of yet. And the parents do facilitate the expression of certain personality traits. That does depend on them. But once again, the parents themselves can't facilitate the development of personality traits they don't possess themselves. So, it's a losing battle to try to develop something in your child that you haven't yet developed in yourself. Of course, all parents feel that they make some personal contribution to their child's fate. I don't know whether that's good or bad, but that's just the way it is. We all imagine that we're in control. When the child grows up and becomes a proper member of society, then the parents often say they've "given him a proper upbringing." If he never turns into anything, the best we'll say of the parents is that they "didn't keep an eye on him." But one's character is constructed out of so many tiny psycho-emotional threads whose growth doesn't depend on us at all, that it would be a mistake to give parents much credit for forming their child's character. We're powerless in this arena. The mechanism of a growing organism's interactions with the outside world is so huge, that it's simply not possible to control every emotion that comes up, just as it's impossible to develop any given set of emotions. We can point to more than one instance in which the parents tried to surround a child with only positive things and protected him from anything negative, but he nonetheless grew into a cruel and unprincipled person. It's the same in the case of parents who tried to inculcate their child with cruelty, in the hope of raising a dictator, but – as if to spite everyone – the future dictator grew up kind-hearted and compassionate. One's personality is the way it is, and it would be a mistake to try to change it in some way. If you bear this in mind, then you might make mistakenly think of the whole question of upbringing this way: if we can't do anything and can't be the foreman directing the construction of our child's personality, then there's no point at all in talking about upbringing. What do we need all these books and advice and discussions for? Well, first of all, the huge empire of psychologists needs something to occupy their time. They develop tests, study how the personality, our "I", the ego, the superego, and the subconscious are constructed. It goes without saying that all of this is interesting and useful, especially for parents who, primarily because of their own personality traits, have a difficult time in their interaction with their children. And children who, for a range of reasons, feel pressured and uncomfortable interacting with their parents also need all of this. We're not all born smart, mature and wise. We all make mistakes. And the mistakes we make with our children are particularly painful, because children can't stand up to us adults, can't resist when we terrorize them and want to mold them into something. They can't yet defend themselves; they haven't learned to do that yet. Because they're CHILDREN. And it's quite likely they'll repeat these very same mistakes with their own children. For this reason, if the parents, due to their own ignorance, have belittled a child in every way possible, and have succeeded in lowering his self-esteem, then a psychologist really can help a great deal. If a parent doesn't manage to establish a harmonious relationship with a child because the parent himself is aggressive or controlling, then once again, then a psychologist's methods can provide the family with genuine support. Even so, it's always up to the adults to take the first step toward improving relations. There's no point in waiting for the child to change or grow up or understand. If you do, you can end up spending your whole life waiting for that and never get it. Every day and every moment in our interactions with our children is precious. Time passes without a trace, and we waste it on fighting with each other, spend it on our desires and on whatever else we want, on anything but interacting with our children. When I say "interacting," I don't just mean uttering the words, "Are you going to eat?" or "How are things in school?" I mean interacting on the level of "I'm and person and you're a person," i.e., the equal, friendly, open, united interactions of people who are building a happy, joyful life together, people who, even when trouble strikes, with always have support. In other words, a Family. If we assert that you can't construct a personality, can't remake or change it, then that definitely doesn't mean that the need for child-rearing vanishes. Yes, I am more than convinced that we're powerless to do anything with either our or anyone else's personality. But child-rearing does have a place in our relationships with our children, as an element of the process of establishing habits.

You'll often hear a parent, particularly a dad, say this when the topic of his son comes up in conversation: "Now, my parents didn't read me any books, and I turned out just fine. And I'll raise my son the same way." We can rest assured that the son will grow up, and it's possible that he'll grow into no worse a person than his father-teacher. However, in our technology-laden century, in this century of anxiety and hysteria, of no time and racing to earn money, we shouldn't rely on "it's possible." A hundred years ago, children were nurtured with the energy of nature. They – and their parents, too, by the way – were calmer, more even tempered, and harmonious. People were closer to nature. They didn't experience the kinds of stresses contemporary man feels, and as a result, they felt less irritated by their children. Children had more freedom, because giving a child freedom didn't mean putting him in danger the way it does today. Maybe this is why people have begun paying so much attention lately to questions of upbringing. How can we keep our children safe without limiting their freedom? How can we teach our children kindness when there's nothing but cruelty on television? How can we keep from shouting at our children when our nerves get so frayed at work? So, today's educators and psychologists face a difficult task in trying to find answers to these questions.

Over-Sheltering

A mom is waking her son up:
"Mikey! Get up! Time to go to school!"
"Mom, I don't want to."
"Mikey! Wake up or you'll be late!"
Mikey sits up and says,
"Mom, there are at least two reasons
I can't go to school:
First of all, no one there likes me,
And second of all, I don't like anyone there."
"Mikey, there are at least two reasons
you need to go to school:
First of all, you're 40 years old, and second of all – you're the principal!"

In our interactions with children we often confuse the two concepts of loving and sheltering. Very often, if we're sheltering or fussing over our children too much, if we want to shield them from unpleasantness, it's because we love them. Parents' love for their children is so blind that they don't see how this can harm a developing personality. More often than not, this kind of blind love actually destroys the children. Love in and of itself can't bring harm, assuming it's a reasonable, non-egotistical love. One day I happened to witness the following conversation between a mom and her child. The little boy was playing in the sandbox, and the mom came up and said, "It's time to go home." The child looked at his mom and asked, "Oh, is it time to eat already?" "No," the mom answered. "You're frozen." In other words, the mom is totally living this child's life for him. She decides when he should eat, what he should wear, who he can play with and for how long. All of this seems totally harmless when the child is still little. In such cases, for the most part, the parents aren't very demanding of the child, everyone plays by the rules, and no particular conflicts arise. But the problems begin as the child gets older. Parents get so into playing the role of loving guardians that they strive to live the child's entire life for him, while of course masquerading as loving and caring parents. I remember a totally horrifying incident involving a family from Russia. The parents raised their daughter and wanted only the very best for her in every way, which is, of course, natural for loving parents. The little girl grew up very obedient, totally trusting her parents and their decisions. She simply didn't know any other way to live. She didn't know how to offer resistance, because after all, her parents had decided things her whole life, and they wanted only the best for her. So, the rebel in her remained asleep. It came time for her to get married. And the parents decided that the local boys couldn't hold a candle to their beautiful daughter. She was a queen to them and deserved only the best. The daughter went off to school to study foreign languages, and her parents began looking for a smart, rich and generous man for her to marry. If that's what you're looking for, of course, you'll need to get married three times, because you'll never find all three in one person. But evidently the parents didn't know this, and they wouldn't give up hope of finding the sole "three-in-one" candidate who would make their daughter happy for her whole life. They found him. Abroad, naturally. Because of course their daughter shouldn't live in poor, coarse, cold Russia. She should live on the seashore. They found this foreign prince on the Internet. He was rich and only ten years older than the queen herself. "No problem. A husband should be older. It's even better that way," said the mother, the wise voice of experience. The fiancé came to the Russian sticks to meet his fiancée. He brought along a video of his house, and gifts for everyone, and he amazed everyone with his sense of humor and his generosity. Only he turned out not to be ten years older, but a full twenty. What's more, in his photos he was in good shape, but in real life he was overweight. He explained that he'd put up an old photo on the Internet because he hadn't had a more recent one. The fiancée didn't like her fiancé. He was old, fat and unattractive. But the parents said, "You'll like him when you get used to him. Why stay here in Russia and dry up?" The obedient little girl offered no resistance – if that's what her parents wanted, it was for the best. The fiancé took his bride off to faraway America. A year later the daughter came back and said she wasn't going anywhere else ever. She didn't love him. Her husband had turned out to be very greedy and jealous; he'd beat her and wouldn't let her leave the house. Not long after, the spouse himself arrived. He begged her to come back, videotaped every single day they spent together in Russia. He recorded everything: when he'd bring her flowers, when he'd go down on his knees, when he'd declare his love for her and try to convince her to come back, because he couldn't imagine life without her. And at this point the parents butted in again: "Go on, sweetheart. Maybe everything will work out. He loves you. He's asking you to forgive him. Try a fresh start. One needs to be able to forgive." The parents appealed to her to forgive him, but not to love him. One needs to marry for love, and if you do, then everything will fall into place, including forgiveness. And once again, the daughter didn't dare to disobey her parents, because they were trying everything to help her. The couple left. That was the last time the parents saw their daughter. It turned out that the groom needed the whole performance, the one he'd recorded on video, as proof of his love for her. Later on, this tape was also used for his defense in court. Before he'd come to Russia to bring his wife back, he'd already hired a friend to murder her. It turned out that her husband was mentally ill, with low self-esteem, which he would raise by collecting young and beautiful wives. This girl was a beauty. They found her disfigured body in a garage. An interview with her mom aired on TV. The woman was crying and asking her daughter for forgiveness, after the fact. She said she'd wanted only the best for her. Admitted having made some mistakes. She'd pressured her daughter, insisted, wanting only the best possible future for her daughter. This sad story helps us see clearly that by living our children's lives for them, we make them defenseless, helpless, weak-willed, incapable of making decisions and taking responsibility for their own lives. If this girl's parents had taught her to love, and above all, to love herself, then she never would have condemned herself to that marriage. One has to be terribly unloving toward oneself and one's body in order to deprive oneself of the very best thing a woman can experience in her life: love for a man.

Parents get so focused on keeping their children safe that they lose sight of the most important thing: loving their child. Or more precisely, without even realizing it, we substitute one idea for the other: we think that by sheltering our children, we're loving them. This becomes particularly harmful as the child matures. The parents demand good grades and push their children into universities and colleges, deciding for them what professions to choose. Then they complain that their child doesn't want to study. Of course he won't study. As popular wisdom tells us, "you can lead a horse to water, but you can't make it drink."

We shouldn't be afraid of giving our children some independence. In practice, this means interfering in our children's business less. That doesn't mean we let everything slide – it goes without saying that there needs to be some control. Trust, but check. But as we loosen our vigilance, we also teach the child to take responsibility for his own affairs. For example, you can constantly follow your child around and say, "Have you done your homework?" and "Did you put everything in your backpack?" and "Do you have your lunch?" and "Did you pick up your toys?" Or you can put together a list of his morning and evening jobs and hand all of it over to your child. He'll be happy to walk around with the list and check off everything he's done and note what he hasn't. At the end of the day you do have to go and check whether he's done everything, and help him with what remains undone. But if you constantly help him, he'll count on the help. If a child consistently has trouble getting something done, then in that case, you can make up a second list in which you note the jobs he can do on his own and the one you'll do together. Make up the list together with your child. Make a deal with him that every week you'll move one job from the "do this together" column to the "do this yourself" column. Your child will like this kind of little game and will help him learn to do everything on his own more quickly.

It's easy to entrust small jobs to your child, but it's a more complicated matter to allow him independence in larger matters. Here you have to be willing to incur "losses." But as a result of doing this, the child will learn to see the negative consequences of his shortcomings. And that's the most priceless thing. When he comes face to face with the consequences of his own shortcomings, the child matures, learns to take responsibility, and grows stronger and more confident (assuming, of course, he's not punished by his parents for his mistakes with a slap in the face.) This is why, when we hand a job over to a child, we should be prepared to incur slight losses. I remember a story about one mother whose young daughter wanted to do something nice for her by doing the laundry. She loaded both lights and darks into the washing machine. She was so proud to announce that she'd washed and dried all the laundry. The mother took one look at the white laundry that had turned blue and praised her daughter for her creative approach to the laundry, and for taking initiative. Fortunately, that mom was ready to lose a little. The next time, they did the laundry together.

Extreme and ongoing sheltering of children prevents them from growing up. By placing responsibility for their matters on children, we teach them self-sufficiency, determination and courage. That is the greatest love we can show them. Extreme sheltering and shielding infantilize them socially, which leads to a host of other problems: insecurity, an inability to cope with life's difficulties, hostility toward the world, and as a result, they end up feeling unhappy, useless, and alone.

We need to show concern – by helping, directing, correcting and exercising control. And we need to show love, just not through excessive sheltering. One of the things our child needs most is, in fact, for us to show him our love. Satisfying that need is a necessary condition for normal development. But we satisfy that need by letting our child know that he's dear to us, that we need him, that we love him. We satisfy that need when we hug and caress him. But not when we do all his work for him, not when we live his life, and not when we protect him from making mistakes in every way possible. The negative effects of these well-meaning actions will make themselves known in the child's adult life.

A child will pick up on love even when the parent meets him with a loving glance, and he'll also see it when you say, "I'm so glad we have you," or "I'm glad to see you," or "It's so good that you're home," and in our actions. He'll see it in all that you do, because he's looking for it. What struck me in my work with abandoned children living in orphanages is how much children love their moms. Maybe she beat him, or sent him out into the freezing cold to beg and then took the money to buy herself a bottle of vodka, or locked him in the apartment hungry, or even forgot he existed at all. Even so, the first chance he gets, he'll run away from the orphanage and go to her, because she's alone there and she's in bad shape. The child will say, "She's a good person and she loves me. She just drinks some vodka sometimes." He prefers to be beaten and hungry yet again, if only he can be with her. There are many such stories. When a child is young, there's no way he'll turn his back on his mother, no matter what, which is more than you can say about mothers. They'll give up their children, sometimes even bringing them to the orphanages themselves, saying, "It'll be better for him here. He'll be fed and warm." And it's a good thing that they bring them. It's only that the child doesn't feel that way. He needs his mother's love more than he needs a piece of bread and a roof over his head.

Even when you punish a child you need to do it with love. You can be annoyed on the outside, but even then, the child should always be able to feel your love. I write about this in detail in the chapter "Punishment."

Not long ago some psychologists studied hugs. They determined that children who receive up to 4 or 5 hugs a day from their parents are more talented, and that their talent often approaches the genius level. For example, Virginia Satir recommends that we hug our children several times a day, since they need at least four hugs a day simply to survive. And to feel good, they need at least eight!

Spoiling

"Yes, Bobby, we've spoiled you...
I guess we'll have to punish you!"
"What d'ya mean? YOU did the spoiling, and I get punished?"

Developmental psychology's treatment of spoiling is somewhat contradictory. This is perhaps the most controversial question developmental psychologists have ever faced. Parents often confuse spoiling with being loving. For example, it seems to them that we're showing our love, when in fact, we're spoiling the child. Or the opposite happens: it seems to us that the child isn't getting enough love (this often happens in incomplete families,)and we want to show our love in some way, so we end up buying him some toy or other, because we can't manage to find any better way to do show our love. But sometimes we go to the opposite extreme. The parents are so afraid of spoiling the child that they consider it unacceptable to buy something unless there's a special occasion, even just some little knick-knack. But it's so nice to receive something out of the blue and not just on your birthday or Christmas. For example, when my eldest son was little, every evening when I'd come home from work, I'd bring him a rye bread roll and say, "I just met a bunny on the way home, and he asked me to give you this." We'd always buy a loaf of white and one rye roll, but we always only presented the rye roll as a gift from the bunny. The whole family would eat this roll at dinner and praise the bunny. I continued to bring home this gift from the bunny every day except Saturday and Sunday for many years, until my child grew up. I was convinced that the longer a child believes in miracles, the better. My older son even believed in Santa Claus until he was almost 15. We kept this secret very carefully and were very meticulous in preparing for Santa's visit. Can you call that spoiling? No.

However, is there any reason parents shouldn't "spoil" their children every day with modest little gifts like a bread roll from a bunny? Can such pampering really negatively affect a child's upbringing?

When we talk about spoiling little children, parents often like to bring up the Japanese method of child rearing, which says that up until age five, a child should never hear the words "you can't do that." This period of so-called "all-permissiveness" lasts only until age 5. Up until then, Japanese parents treat their children like "kings"; from 5 to 15 they treat them like "slaves", and from 15 on up, like "equals". The idea is that a fifteen-year-old adolescent is already an adult who is keenly aware of his responsibilities and who obeys the rules impeccably. Herein lies the paradox of Japanese childrearing: a child who was permitted everything in childhood grows into a disciplined and law-abiding citizen. However, many people strive to import this Japanese childrearing model to Western reality, although one should never look at it in isolation from Japanese culture. In Japan, once a child reaches age five, he enters a very rigid system of rules and limitations that function in society. It goes without saying, that Western societies also have their behavioral norms, but these rules are so flexible that a child who's been raised in a totally permissive way until age five won't have the brakes put on him after that. Japan is a country of groups, castes and strict social conventions. Children sense this as soon as they enter society. If you're not like everyone else, you'll have trouble. The goal of Japanese pedagogy is to raise a person who will fit into society. Our goals are somewhat different, and so our educational methods will be different, too. We focus on developing individuality. We welcome any type of thought, whether it's usual or unusual. And incidentally, some Japanese pedagogues have begun talking about the deficiencies of Japanese child-rearing methods: a shift toward group consciousness gradually leads to the inability to think independently. Moreover, the idea of sticking to one unified standard becomes so deeply rooted in children's consciousness, that if one of them expresses his own personal opinion, then he immediately becomes a pariah, the object of ridicule, or even hatred. This phenomenon also occurs in our schools; we call it bullying. The reasons for it can take any form, but they often have nothing to do with a child expressing his individuality.

Something that's genuinely unique and relevant for our society is the attitude that's inculcated in Japanese children toward their mother from the time they're born. Children call their moms "amae". It's hard to come up with a precise English translation of this word. It signifies the extremely close bond a child has with his mother. The verb *amaeru* means "to use something", "to be spoiled", "to seek shelter." When a baby is born, the midwife cuts off a piece of the umbilical cord, dries it, and puts it into a traditional wooden box a little bigger than a matchbox. The mother's name and the child's birth date are stamped in gold letters on the box. This is a symbol of the connection between the mother and the infant. You'll rarely see a crying tot in Japan. The mother strives to do everything so that he'll have no reason to cry. For the first year, it's as if the child is still a part of the mother's body: she carries him around all day long, tied to her back, lays him next to her at night to sleep and nurses him whenever he wants. Adults will only warn him, not scold him: "That's hot," "That's dirty," "Watch out." As a rule, children worship their mothers to such an extent that they feel guilty and sorry when they cause them any unpleasantness at all.

Little boys and little girls are raised differently, since they will have to fulfill different social roles. One Japanese proverb says, "A man shouldn't enter the kitchen." The Japanese see the son as the future support of the family. On one of the national holidays, Boys' Day, people hoist representations of multi-colored carps into the air. This fish is capable of swimming against the current for long periods of time, and they symbolize the path of the future man, who's capable of overcoming all of life's difficulties. And the girls are taught to do the housework: to cook, sew, do the wash. You'll see these same differences in child rearing in school. After school, little boys always attend various study groups to continue their learning, while girls are free to hang out in cafes and chat about fashion.

The Japanese never raise their voices to their children and never lecture them, to say nothing of corporal punishment. But they do often say things to them, especially between the ages of 5 and 15, which would be totally unacceptable in our society: "If you keep behaving like that, everyone will laugh at you and you'll end up alone." That's the most terrifying thought for the Japanese, since they can't conceive of themselves outside the collective. From ages 5 to 15, children are taught to seek out their place in society. Otherwise, they can get lost in it, lose their way and live their lives with no purpose. The Japanese have a very difficult time coping with loneliness. Perhaps this is why Japan is among the countries at the top of the list for suicide rates. It's hard for an individual in this country to be on his own – after all, since childhood it's drummed into him that he needs to be a member of society.

As far as spoiling is concerned in our society, it's very important to take the child's age as your guide. For example, when a child is still nursing, it's physical contact with the child that plays a key role. But out of fear of spoiling their child, parents make the most unforgivable mistake: they don't cuddle their child enough. They think that if they pick their child up too often and pamper them with attention and caresses, he'll get spoiled and will constantly ask to be picked up. It's unclear where they got this idea. Are there really children who grow up and continue asking their mom to pick them up? Quite the opposite. The child passes through this developmental phase and begins to ask to be put down whenever his mother tries to pick him up. He wants to take his first steps on his own, he wants to experience his environment himself. So, by not giving the child enough cuddling and love in this developmental period, you're sowing the seeds of lack of confidence and vulnerability in him and cultivating a mass of personality problems. The same is true in regard to the question of whether or not to bring the child into the parents' bed. Many psychologists are quick to recommend that one should never bring the child into one's own bed. He should recognize his own little bed, get used to it and under no circumstances share the parents' bed. Of course, if the child is constantly sleeping with the adults, then that leads to certain problems. He doesn't recognize his own personal space. In particular, it's not advisable for little boys to sleep with their mothers, or little girls with their fathers, since the parents' scent is stored in the child's subconscious, and then later, once he or she becomes sexually active, the boy or girl might unconsciously respond to precisely this scent when seeking a partner. A ban on sleeping in the parents' bed generally applies to children between the ages of 8 and 10. But in the psychological literature, I haven't run across any convincing argument that would support keeping little children out of the parents' bed. Why do we consider that spoiling? Say what you will, but you can't ever have too much cuddling or warmth, or too many hugs. It's impossible to spoil a child this way. How sweet it is to bring a child into the bed and lay him down in the middle and cover him with a giant blanket, sing him a song, or just be silent. Sometimes silence is useful. Beneath his parent's wings, the child feels safe, strong and needed. But at the same time, the child still needs to have his very own bed. It's particularly important to place a child in his own little bed as soon as he comes home from the hospital, to put him in the crib on the very first day, instead of in a stroller or an easy chair or the grown-ups' bed. That way the child will feel that people have been waiting for him there, preparing for his arrival there; he'll feel wanted. He'll know that he has his own space, which however doesn't preclude sometimes placing him under the parents' wing now and again.

It's impossible to spoil a child with too much love. But you *can* ruin a child with all the other things parents mistakenly associate with showing love. For example, indulging a child when it's a matter of over-indulgence instead of need. More than anything else, loving a child means helping him function in life. In other words, through our love we help him construct a world around him in which he can function successfully. But parents very often take loving and taking care of a child to mean fulfilling all of his infantile desires. If you allow the child everything, if the parents do all they can to help him solve his own problems, then we end up with a person who is bound to suffer in his adult life. Once he's grown up, the child very quickly discovers that the world has no intention of adjusting to him. People have no intention of dancing to his tune. This is very disorienting. To a child who's been raised in indulgence, the world seems hostile. The spoiled child is fated to be an outcast. The realities of life are such that no society, and no family, no matter how loving it might be, will take care of him for his whole life. Alfred Adler, who raised four children of his own, has written a great deal about the psychopathology of the spoiled child. His long years of practice in the field of individual psychology have shown that people who suffer from neuroses were spoiled as children. This indulgence creates an abnormal worldview, in which you see all the surrounding people as existing only for you. Everyone owes you something, and what's more, you shouldn't have to make any contribution whatsoever. When we see that a person's incapable of functioning independently, that's proof that he's been spoiled: for example, if a person is in the habit of leaving a mess in his wake, then it follows that he was always surrounded by someone who would continually clean up after him. In some cases, the opposite can be true. A spoiled child might, on the contrary, be very pedantic, once again, if everyone around him was always cleaning everything up. This means that he'll demand constant cleanliness from those around him. But Adler's most interesting observation concerns the great fear that spoiled children experience. This fear is always present in them. As a rule, one finds less fear in children who experienced an insignificant level of spoiling, in children who learned to be independent and learned how to be alone from the time they were young. They're capable of nighttime agitation, or they might throw a tantrum from time to time, but on the whole, they cause their parents fewer problems. In their adult life, we see no serious deviant behavior: they're more harmonious, happier, and fully satisfied with life. By the way, the child who was his parents' favorite can also expect little in the way of future happiness. Spoiling gives birth to a host of psychological problems in adult life.

Also along these lines, one should have a reasonable approach to the gifts one gives one's child. You can take the child's real needs as a good guideline here. What the child always needs, on any given day, is for you to spend time with him, and you can never overdo that. But we often take the path of least resistance. It's so much easier to buy a toy. The child gets very happy when he sees it, excited, but before long he gets sick of it and wants a new one. And in such cases, he needs the new toy not so much as a toy, but rather as an object that will elicit the same positive feelings and impressions he felt before. Of course, the child won't have any inkling of this; he just wants a new toy, and he gets it. But in actual fact, what's he's receiving through it is a dose of new positive emotions. What's happening is like an emotional substitution. Instead of receiving positive emotions from interacting with the surrounding world, the child receives these emotions from the toy. Perhaps it isn't a big difference, but over time the child will start demanding more and more new toys, and what's more, he'll continue this pursuit once he's grown, only the toys will already be grown-up toys that won't always be harmless, and there will never be enough of them.

We love buying toys, since we enjoy making our child happy. We like to see the child's joyful eyes and his excitement. It's like compensation for having spent our day at work. But no toy can replace 20-30 minutes of role-playing play with a child. I'm not urging parents to stop buying toys in general. However, I *am* against buying toys on demand. I would often buy my children toys. But I don't think I ever did that on demand, much less make a deal such as "you'll get a toy for good behavior, for good grades, for cleaning up at home," etc. There are toys in our home, but they were all purchased on the spur of the moment, as a surprise, not in connection with any occasion. The only exception is toys presented on birthdays or Christmas. The child especially looks forward to those toys, sometimes even making requests. Giving toys as a surprise isn't spoiling. It's not bowing to his wishes, not making a deal with a child, or fulfilling his whims. It's something that comes from the heart.

In summing up, I'd like to stress that we do need to indulge our children. Indulge them with our attention, our interaction, our presence, and our caresses. That's the most harmless indulgence we can possibly offer. Many parents believe you need to give all of this to boys only in very small doses, since they are future men. They shouldn't cry, and they need less cuddling. Total lies. It's precisely when boys receive too little cuddling in the form of embraces, kisses and similar expressions of tenderness that they hang out with loose women once they're adults. The reason for most emotional disturbances and failures in adult life is a shortage of love.

In this age of frenzied pursuit, of parents who work for days at a time, in this age of children who are raised solely by cell phone, many parents feel guilty for spending too little time with their children. For this reason they go to the opposite extreme when it comes to indulgence. They can't find anything better to do on their rare day off than head to the store to buy toys. While raising my own children, I also worked a lot and was never a stay-at-home mom. But by the same token, I've become firmly convinced that you can spend the entire day with a child and give him nothing. But you can spend just an hour a day with a child and pour so much into him in the course of that hour that he'll look forward to the next hour more than he would to any toy.

Money

**Attention, parents! You know your child has grown up if, when you ask, "What should I give you?"
he replies, "Give me money."**

Lately it's become popular to give a child pocket money. When we moved to Canada, nearly every child in the school already had pocket money by the time he was in third grade. Our son also began asking us to give him an allowance that he could save if he didn't spend it. His classmates were receiving $5-$10 from their parents every week. Because we had rather conservative views on this topic, we didn't start giving him a weekly allowance, so that this wouldn't turn into some kind of tradition or obsession. But we began giving him a little money from time to time, so that he wouldn't feel uncomfortable in his group of classmates. But to this day I don't understand what people mean by pocket expenses for a ten-year old. The child doesn't go anywhere on his own, doesn't buy anything, and in elementary schools there aren't even any vending machines where he could buy snacks or water. So what does that child need pocket money for? But you can't argue with parents' habit of spoiling their children in every way possible. All you can do is simply accept the societal norms and adjust to them.

When a child is in the higher grades, parents tend to encourage the student's success by offering him financial rewards. Maybe it works all right. I don't know. We never used that method. It seems to me that sooner or later, the child will start demanding more and more, while doing less and less, and without putting in the necessary effort and creativity. Our family often used a different method to encourage the children in their studies. If they had a successful academic year, then in the summer we'd buy them a new bicycle or some technology, like an iPod. Maybe that's the same as giving them money, but in our family, the children never received money directly. The only exception was birthdays, when relatives would take the easier route and give him money instead of fussing with a present. Another exception was games in which the winner would receive a small monetary equivalent of a prize. But in this case, it was as if the child was earning this money through his focus or erudition. As far as birthday presents are concerned, we're used to giving something other than money. We prepare a gift beforehand, bearing the child's interests in mind. If you've thought this gift through well, if you've presented it with a sense of humor, if it's not just a gift for the sake of giving a gift, but something the child wants and can use, then a year later, when you ask whether you should give him money for his birthday or come up with a present, he'll choose the present without a second thought. We began asking our older child whether he'd like money or a gift beginning roughly at age 15. We don't ask our younger son – he usually beats us to it and requests a gift long before his birthday. True, he changes his request every time he sees an ad for a new toy on a TV. As a result, by the time his birthday rolls around, a whole list appears with crossed out toy names, and it's constantly being updated with new toys. But with our older son, since he turned 15, we find out whether he'd like money for his birthday, so that he can buy something on his own, or a gift of our choosing. If he picks the gift, then we don't discuss it, and he doesn't know what we'll come up with, so it ends up being a surprise. The amount we spend on the gift is equivalent to the amount we would have given him if he'd chosen the money. And it feels very nice that almost every year, our son chooses the gift over the money. This shows that we hit the mark the previous year, that our choice suited his tastes.

It's no simple matter to choose a gift for a child. The task gets more difficult with every year, as he matures. It's easy with little tykes – they'll be happy with any toy. But adolescents are very picky. They still have a strong desire to imitate their peers. They want to have what others have, to fit into the crowd, but to also stand out in it, too. Sometimes they want the impossible. To us adults, it seems that they're trying going in two directions at once. For example, they want to have everything others have, but at the same time they want what they have to be different from what others have. In general, it's a case of "I'm going somewhere, but I don't know where," of "Give me this, but I don't know what I want." For this reason, when you're faced with the question of what to buy an adolescent for a birthday present, you have to take a multitude of factors into account, such as what he's interested in at the moment, his capabilities, and even his social group. We try to approach this process with creativity and a sense of humor. For example, if we're giving a small item, then we wrap it in the biggest box we can find. We usually do a combination gift: working within the sum of money we've set aside for the gift, we'll buy several small things we think he can use at the moment. Sometimes we buy him one thing. But the gifts should never be connected to the child's achievements or work. It's better if they're related to what he enjoys. After all, it's a present, and it should bring pleasure. For example, don't give a child a book if he doesn't like to read. I understand grown-ups' noble impulse to give a child an encyclopedia or a clever game to develop his mind, to introduce him to learning. The only problem is, will the child appreciate it? It's like giving your wife a state-of-the-art iron. Of course, it's a necessary household item, but it's something she uses to do work. Maybe it's not a bad gift in and of itself, for when you just feel like giving a present, but it'll never be a hit as a birthday gift. By the way, some men have even had the bright idea of giving their wives irons and vacuum cleaners after an argument, as a way to make up. And the most interesting thing is that sometimes it works! It makes me wonder what the old iron must have been like if she's so happy to get the new one.

As far as gifts for adolescents are concerned, you could give stylish clothing, electronics, or musical instruments, again depending on the child's interests. For example, when I was looking for a gift for my son's fifteenth birthday, I came across a photo on the Internet of his favorite (at the time) singer, the leader of a popular rock band. We ordered a T-shirt with that photo on it, and underneath the photo we signed "To Elvin from his idol." He was beside himself with delight. His first question was, "Where did you find this?" We've come up with other interesting presents, too. One time we did a Photoshop collage: we combined a picture of our son with a picture of his friend and then Photoshopped the boys into a photo of their favorite rappers. That way in the final photo they were in amongst their idols. We took this final edit to the photo store, and they printed it onto mugs for us. We couldn't have imagined a better Christmas gift.

One should use a creative approach to everything, but this is especially true when you're choosing gifts. I really like the process of picking out a gift, and not just for kids, but for adults, too. I never give anyone money. To me that feels like the most empty gift you can give. Many people give money because they don't have the time to wander through the stores. It's so much simpler to give a gift card, but it seems to me that even an ordinary flower in a pot will mean more than a banknote in an envelope. Of course, not all gifts are a hit, and you have to be prepared for that. You can't always guess size or color or tastes correctly. But it's the process of choosing itself that's important, the attention you give to the person as you're looking for a gift for him, and the moment when you present it. It's always seemed to me that giving a gift is far more interesting than receiving one.

Speaking of money, I want to tell you about a family we often spend time with. I really enjoy being at their house, because when you're there you enter a world where love and understanding reign. That's as clear as day, even to the unaided eye. I particularly like their approach to money. It's a family of six children, three girls and three boys. The father owns two stone factories and is always ends up staying late at work. The mom does the majority of the child rearing, with the help of a nanny. The family is very well off and can afford lots of things. But they only recently got a computer at home, which they use mainly for Skyping. The children have no state-of-the-art electronics, cool cell phones or iPods. They have all the essentials, including a personal driver, since they go to a private school far from home. But they don't have more than they need. The father has a straightforward position on this question: "If they want a fancy expensive phone, I'm not against it, but they have to earn at least 20 percent of the cost themselves. I'll happily contribute the other 80 percent if they don't manage to earn the entire sum over the summer. But they should earn the things that are for amusement." In this family, the father's word is the law. His pronouncements aren't discussed or subject to doubt. The mother has a vote, and she has authority, and she's fully capable of disagreeing or arguing with her husband. After all, no matter how much the rooster crows, it's the hen that lays the eggs. But the children will never witness these disagreements. In this family with its modern Western bent, the wife in some magical way still manages to combine Eastern female submissiveness with strength and wisdom. Sure, they buy their children gifts, even expensive ones sometimes, if there's an occasion. But there aren't many gifts like that. The children really like playing with each other, inventing various role-playing games, competitions and the like. One time I had the chance to see what happened when the phone rang while one of these games was in full swing. The wife picked up the phone without even a glance at the children. Instantly, as if she'd waved a magic wand, stillness reigned in the house. The children fell silent. The father was calling to see how everything was. Once the mother was done talking, the ear-splitting din rose again. That's just the way those children had been raised.

Punishment

Bobby tells the classmate sitting next to him,
"My dad spanked me twice yesterday."
"What for?"
"The first time was when I showed him my report card. You should have seen the grades and bad teacher's notes! The second time was when he realized that was *his* old report card."

Another of the most controversial topics in child rearing is punishment. Can we raise children without punishment? Many people assert that the correct way to approach child rearing is to do without punishment. Perhaps. But our family isn't one of the ones that doesn't use punishment. To be perfectly honest, I've yet to meet a family in which there was absolutely no punishment. There are obedient children, disobedient children, and somewhat obedient children (although, what do you mean by "somewhat"?) But there's no such thing as parents who don't ask anything of their children, including obedience. There are parents who don't give their children as much attention as they should, but even they can be masters at telling a child to do things. Punishment comes into play if we tell a child to do something and he doesn't do it. For this reason, I'd divide child educators – and all parents fall into this category – into two groups. The first group (and this represents the majority) includes parents who are actively engaged in bringing up their children. They do the best they can with it. Sometimes they act intuitively, which is the best way to approach this task, sometimes they learn from their mistakes, but sometimes they don't learn anything at all. Nonetheless, they manage to give the child what he needs. They pay attention to him, interact with him and help him. They're always at the ready, always on hand to lend their child a helping hand when he really needs it. Parents of this kind will require their children to do well in school, to behave reasonably, to be obedient, and so on. And rightly so. There's also a second group of parents, and it seems to me that they're in the minority, or at least I really want to believe they are. These are the parents who pay no attention whatsoever to their child. There can be a whole range of reasons for this: illness, work, problems in their personal life, etc. But although they don't have time for child rearing, they always do find time to place demands on their children. Such parents are actually often extremely demanding of their children when it comes to school, behavior, habits, etc. Perhaps even more demanding than the first type of parents. Because of this, once their children hit adolescence, these parents go through a period of lack of understanding and conflicts with the children. The children complain that the parents don't get them, while the parents grumble that it's a difficult age, and that they're helpless. Where do these parents think they're going to get this understanding if they haven't been involved in raising the child, if they haven't experienced all the moments of his life with him, thereby growing too, as a result? A Russian proverb says, "Blinder than blind, stupider than stupid is the one who hasn't educated his kid." In families in which the parents have passed through all stages of a child's life alongside him, have witnessed his difficulties and victories, his ascents and falls – because children do go through all of this, too – the adolescent period will pass more smoothly. Parents will be able to resolve any disagreements that do arise without being stubborn, by using great love and understanding. As a general rule, once children hit adolescence, punishment no longer works. In spite of this, this is exactly the period when parents turn to punishment more often than ever before. It's a paradox. But they use punishment because it seems to them nothing else works any more. That's one of the most glaring errors one can make, because during this phase when a child is most in need of love, he also ends up getting punished. This is terribly disrespectful, but it's exactly what many parents do. When an adolescent isn't getting enough love, this turns into "they don't understand me." Meanwhile, our adult vision doesn't always pick up on the fact that the adolescent is feeling this lack of love. At the tip of the iceberg all you can see is mutual misunderstanding. So imagine what can happen if, on top of everything else – in addition to increased criticism of his appearance, in addition to his anxiety, to his adolescent lack of confidence, to his feeling that he's an adult, and to feeling he's not getting enough love – he's also bombarded with punishment by his parents. You get a damaged individual with a host of issues, with low self-esteem, and without will power, etc. For this reason, I'd take punishment off the table entirely, along with active child rearing, too, because by this point the child already has a fully formed character and habits. There's no reason to try to educate him. What's been laid down in him has been laid down. The only thing an adolescent needs at this age is his parents' help. And he's likely to reject even that in most cases. I write in more detail about interactions between parents and adolescent children in the chapter "The Adolescent."

As far as punishment is concerned, maybe rare parents who manage without it do exist. But as I wrote above, I haven't met any. If you tell your child to do things, then you'll use punishment, too, because a child who's developing normally, whose will has not yet been broken by his parents, will never unquestioningly do absolutely everything his parents tell him to do. If the child's will is already broken, then the parents might be able to avoid resorting to punishment. But this is nothing to be proud of. Don't congratulate yourself on your great child raising skills. If the child no longer resists and obeys the parents in every way, it means that there's been so much punishment that the child is simply exhausted; he's given up; he's broken. This isn't a normal state of affairs, and it means you need to review your approach to child rearing. Children shouldn't unquestioningly submit to their parents in everything. That isn't normal. It's totally natural for them not to do what they're asked, or to do it in their own way, or to be slow to carry out their tasks, to ignore their responsibilities. Because we're the same way. However, totally disregarding the parents' requests and systematically avoiding carrying out one's responsibilities should also prompt you to take a look at the system you're using to raise your children.

When we talk about punishment we often mean corporal punishment, but tend to underestimate the consequences of our unreasonable shouting and insults, both of which constitute emotional punishment.

I am against physical punishment, and I'm just as opposed to emotional punishment. Our family has a system of punishment that, I'm sorry to say, we use fairly frequently. Evidently, we didn't cultivate the necessary habits in our children, habits that would have grown, as the children grew older, into responsibilities and necessary behaviors. For this reason, we have to resort to punishment more often than we'd like. But our system of punishment excludes corporal punishment. All of our methods of punishment are based on one idea: deprivation of something enjoyable. If the child doesn't do something he knew he was supposed to do, then as soon as I announce, "I'll have to punish you," we usually have a chat. I offer the child the chance to choose his own punishment. Believe me, the fairest punishment is always one the child chooses himself. If the child feels he's done wrong, he'll never give himself a light sentence. He's deprived of fun activities, usually for two days, or for a week, depending on the severity of the act. We're the ones to determine how many days the punishment will last, but the child himself decides which actual enjoyable activity will be excluded. The most severe punishment in our family is not being able to play computer games for the specified time period. Punishment can also include no PlayStation, no access to Xbox, not being allowed to watch favorite cartoons, or confiscation of certain toys, etc. Each child has certain forms of entertainment that he enjoys. If a given job that should have been done isn't done, then the child is deprived of that enjoyment, since after all, pleasure should come after work. There's a time to work, and a time to play. This system of punishment suits us, and it works well. The children know what to expect, and they can always choose whether to carry out their responsibilities or be deprived of what they enjoy. Children really dislike being deprived of their entertainment, as do adults, by the way. So, more often than not, when children disregard their responsibilities, it's not because they don't mind being punished, but because they're forgetful. A child will never consciously choose losing entertainment over carrying out his responsibilities. He might simply forget about them.

And of course, one can forgive forgetfulness. But the chances that the child won't forget about them the next time are zero. He'll still forget again, and he'll continue to forget until he spends a week without his computer or without something else he enjoys. For this reason, I'm of the mind that taking away enjoyment is the most rational form of punishment. But it should also be within reason. You can't take away a child's favorite toy for an extended period. You can't leave him behind on his own if the whole family's going out to do something fun. If the child's done something wrong, it's best to rearrange the plans and for everybody to stay home, but without blaming the child for the fact that the outing didn't take place. You can't send the child off to his grandma – if he doesn't want to go – only because you're sure there won't be anything entertaining for him to do there. We did use this approach at one time, but quickly realized how mistaken that kind of punishment is. One thing we've never done is to use work as punishment. One day our neighbor stopped by and, seeing our youngest child, who was 7 at the time, washing the floor, asked me with surprise, "What did he manage to do wrong so early in the morning? Are you punishing him?" I thought that was really funny. Many people really do associate children doing work with punishment. I told her that the child himself had asked for a bucket of water and wanted to wash the floor. For him, at that moment, that was an original way of entertaining himself. He immediately began playing with the mop and chatting away there in a quiet voice. It never even entered my head that you could punish a child this way. It's unacceptable to punish a child by making him work, because then in the future, the child will associate any form of work with punishment. He'll come to hate work. You also shouldn't levy punishment after the fact for acts that you didn't assign punishment for on the spot. In this case, more than any other time, it's important not to let time lapse. You can tell a child that he'll be punished and that you'll talk about it with him that evening. But if you don't do it that evening, there's no point in doing it retroactively. You can't punish a child for being scared, for being clumsy, for not knowing how to do something, or for not managing a task he just wasn't personally up to. You shouldn't punish a child when you're in a lousy mood, when you're irritated, or when something's wrong that has nothing to do with the child. In such cases your anger will prevent you from determining whether or not the child is guilty, or his motives for not doing the job he'd been given. And when you're scolding a child for something, you shouldn't make it personal, by saying, "You're bad," or "You're irresponsible," or "You're lazy." The act might be bad or the approach might be irresponsible or laziness might come over him through no fault of his own, but the child himself is always the same. You shouldn't punish him right before bed, either. And there's also no point in assailing a child with complaints as soon as he gets up in the morning, even if in the middle of the night you tripped over the toys he hadn't picked up and bruised your nose. The same goes for when the child's eating. If the child's done something and, once you think about it, you're not sure whether or not to punish him, then don't punish him. And there should always only be one punishment. If the child commits several acts that you consider unforgivable, the punishment can be severe, but still only single, not like multiple Xerox copies. Really, what's most important is the way you approach punishing a child. More often than not, we punish our children when we ourselves are annoyed. It's our nature. Of course, under ideal circumstances, it would make more sense to take some time to cool off, to think everything through and then talk with the child. But in actual practice this usually doesn't work. We dole out punishment when we're all worked up. At times like these, parents might slap a child's bottom, shout at him and say, "I'm punishing you!" And that's totally normal, because we're talking emotions here. We can't do anything about our emotions. It would be abnormal if we were to walk away, calm ourselves and then come back and coldly slap a child. I'm not saying that these emotions are good. I'm just saying that they simply exist. We're helpless when it comes to controlling them. You can read a bunch of smart books or go through anger management training, but when an emotion comes up, all the books and clever advice fade into the background. Emotions are very powerful. We can't control our emotions; either they're there or they're not. And this depends totally on the individual features of our character, on our psychological makeup, on heredity and on a lot of other things. There are parents who won't be thrown off by even a dozen disobedient children, and there are parents who fly off the handle at the slightest thing, even if they have only one child. So, I'd like to go into a little more detail about how to handle punishment in cases when our emotions take the upper hand. And this happens quite often. I myself am a very emotional mom, and in spite of my years of meditation, of practice, and using the technique of watching myself, when it comes to my children, I can be just as anxious, emotional, occasionally demanding, and so on, as I was before. In such cases, when you're thinking about punishment, your emotions are not your best friends, but you have to make your peace with this. So, no matter now angry you may get at your child, there's one simple rule you can use, one that will eventually become a habit for you: before you unleash your anger at your child, or in the moments between fits of anger, or even after a fit – whenever you can manage it – definitely tell your child, "I love you." I may shout at you, punish you, and curse, but I love you. Any punishment should be delivered with love. Make sure the child understands that you've already forgiven him, that the punishment doesn't mean lack of forgiveness or reflect your feelings toward him in any way. You're angry, but that doesn't at all mean that you don't love him at that moment and don't forgive him. Punishment is not a way to absolve a child from guilt, and not a step toward forgiveness. It is only a method that will help a child develop self-discipline. It is in no way connected to your feelings for each other. You love him, at all times, regardless of whether he's made his bed or not, regardless of whether he's done his schoolwork or not. But punishment is necessary because it helps a child learn to approach his obligations responsibly. You can explain by drawing an analogy to your obligations. After all, your boss punishes you if you don't do what you're supposed to do. It has nothing to do with feelings.

As far as corporal punishment goes, to this day it's still a fairly widespread method in certain families. In the families that use it, it's seen as the only method that still has some effect. Once they use force on their child, then parents for some reason become convinced that he won't understand anything except force. This is a profound misunderstanding. Our best partners in educating or re-educating our children are discussion, explanation, motivation, patience, and affection. I don't believe that physical punishment is effective. I think it's admissible only in cases where the parent has lost control over his emotions. If the father can't control himself and slaps a child on the ear, or a mom whacks his bottom, that's normal. I'm not saying it's good. Again, it's a question of emotion: it's an explosion that the parents couldn't avert. But if the parents decide to corporally punish a child in a thought-out, intentional way – for example, if they make him stand in the corner or sit locked in a dark room – then that's barbaric and unacceptable. And by the way, a child who experiences excessively strict punishment will begin to feel depressed. The child will seek to relieve his suffering, subconsciously avoiding the source of this suffering. Thus, girls who have suffered at the hands of a volatile father adopt a habit when they're adults of dismissing men on the grounds that they're volatile. Or boys whose strict mothers continually placed psychological pressure on them might avoid women. This avoidance approach can also express itself differently: for example, a child might become timid in his relations with women, or be sexually perverted (which is simply a different way of avoiding women.) Perversion is not innate, but rather develops out of a situation in which a child lives over a period of years. One ends up paying dearly for early childhood mistakes. Nonetheless, parents often don't understand their own life's experience and as a result transfer this mode of behavior to their children, who then repeat their parents' mistakes. Because of this, children often suffer the same fate as their parents and play out the same scenarios. There can be slight variations, but the larger life picture remains the same.

How can one avoid using punishment? Remind your children of their obligations. Always check whether they've completed the work they're assigned. Never forget what jobs you've given them, because if you assign a job and then forget about it, the child will conclude that if you've forgotten about it, it must be an insignificant task. He'll ignore it the next time. Never ask him to do something unreasonable; in other words, never ask him to do something that would be genuinely hard for him to do given his age. Don't ask the child to do something that doesn't really need to be done. And maintain parental solidarity. So for example, the father, no matter how much power he possesses in the family, is not allowed to revoke punishment the mother has imposed. Similarly, the mother shouldn't undermine the father's authority and meddle in his dealings with the children.

It also wouldn't be out of place to stress that in the larger scheme of things, you don't accomplish anything by using punishment. Or more precisely: anything we gain by using punishment is only a temporary concession, a pact. When neither the child nor the adult knows what needs changing, then the education will be fruitless. All the punishment will do is foster secrecy and cowardice in the child, but his approach to life won't change at all. No super strict or super lenient punishments will be able to change him or help establish a positive life experience for him. As the child moves forward, his whole life will play out in accordance with the approach to life he's already developed. We can't facilitate any changes at all unless we touch the core of our child's personality. But if we're going to be able to do that, we have to first of all get a handle on our own core, on our own childhood traumas, understand our own approach to life, what we ourselves feel, and what our own life's goals are. It goes without saying that this requires great personal growth, a huge amount of spiritual work, working on oneself, working on one's inner "I", and closely examining all our egotistical desires and our approach to life.

Relationships

Bobby comes home very sad. His mom asks him,
"Bobby, why are you so sad?"
"Everyone one the playground teases me. They say I have a really big head."
"Bobby, don't pay any attention to those idiots. You'd be better off going to get me some potatoes."
"Give me some kind of bag to use, then."
"What the heck do you need a bag for? Just use your hat – you can fit 10 pounds in it."

The way we interact with our children is another significant topic. We sometimes say something to our children that's so offensive, but without even realizing it. If we could record all of the wrong-headed things we say to our children onto one tape, we'd be shocked at how long it was.

I feel it's important to give our attention to interacting with our children. However, if I analyze my own experience relating to my sons, then I realize that our interactions took shape intuitively, without me using any kind of communicative techniques or guidelines. So, before I began writing this chapter I familiarized myself with the works of child psychologists who've written on the topic of our relations with children. And I learned much of interest. There are special techniques and even phrases that help a child to open up, and help parents grow closer to their children. They offer recommendations on the right way to ask a child questions, and the right way to answer a child's questions. Many of these methods are based in part on the person-centered psychotherapeutic approach, first mentioned by the well-known American psychologist Carl Ransom Rogers.

The gymnastics psychotherapy he proposed (together with Abraham Maslow) turns out to be especially effective in resolving conflicts with difficult children, because it focuses on the personality of the person with whom you're interacting. Thomas Gordon's works on interaction also deserve mention. They're interesting primarily in that they encourage parents to engage in personal development and grow along with their children. His courses go into great detail in teaching parents how to interact.

It goes without saying that all of this is both interesting and educational. It's quite possible that this way of interacting – which is based on using phrases recommended by the psychologists, and which feels unnatural at first – will, if you practice it constantly, transform interacting with your children into a real art. But the take-away I've gotten from my experience interacting with my own children is that what's most valuable is honesty. You can use it in place of any techniques, classes or rules of interaction.

Most conversations between parents and children take place on the fly. We ask our children, on the run, at kind of odd moments, how things are at school, how they spent their day, what they're up to. At the same time, we're getting some food on the table, watching television, glancing at the newspapers and doing a whole other bunch of various things besides the one, most important thing: as we're talking with our child, we're not looking him in the eye. In our family it's been a long-standing tradition to read each other's thoughts by looking at the eyes. Of course, none of us was ever able to do this. But it would always happen that, the moment one of us had the slightest doubt about the other's honesty, we would sagely proclaim, "I can see it in your eyes: you're trying to put one over on me." My children were always convinced that their mother could read their thoughts in their eyes. I'm not sure whether this myth has been debunked now. It's totally possible that it hasn't. But as they've gotten older, they've begun trying to do the same thing themselves, by looking into each other's eyes. They kept pestering me to tell them how to do it. I explained that besides looking into the eyes, their heart and other organs will help them, too. Maybe it's because they believed in my "super powers" (which never existed at all) that my children never made things up. Or at the very least, we never had to deal with lying. We just interacted sincerely and honestly, and, when necessary, we also looked fixedly into their eyes.

  Parents usually have no time to listen to their child. Or, more precisely, we listen, but at times we aren't really engaged in the process. Since we're trapped by our own problems, all our children's problems seem so insignificant and immaterial that the best we're able to come up with is to tell our child, don't worry about it. However, all you need to do in order to have a valuable interaction is just to actively listen. You don't have to give advice or pity your children or blame them. All you need to do is listen. Sometimes silence is more meaningful than action. But you need to listen actively. In other words, the child needs to see that you're interested in what's going on with him. This can backfire when he doesn't want to talk about something and you begin to actively torture it out of him. In that case your interest can play a cruel joke on you. But when your child starts talking about something on his own, then you mustn't ignore it. You shouldn't listen to the child in the middle of things, in passing; you shouldn't flatly intone, "mmhmm, mmhmm" and pretend you're really interested. Children are very sensitive, and some day, when he sense's you're in a hurry or that you're not really interested in his affairs, that you're insincere, he'll stop sharing his thoughts with you. And what's more, when he's a bit older, he'll say, "the older generation doesn't understand a thing."

When relations between family members are open from the very start – i.e., when the husband and wife are capable of having open dialogue with each other – then the child will behave the same way when he's interacting with his parents. You won't have to draw the words out of him, guess what kind of mood he's in, or keep asking him questions. The child will share everything that concerns him with you of his own free will. In such cases, the parents will know all their child's friends well, they'll know all his problems, what's important to him in life, what makes him tick. But if he grows up in a family where – because of family tradition, culture and the relationships between the adults – people aren't used to discussing things with each other in detail, then the child won't do so, either. So, if this is the case, it's important not to build your interactions with your child around questions – because you won't get answers to them anyway. Develop your interactions based on how he's behaving. Let's say your child is upset. You can ask, "What happened?" But 95 out of 100 times the child will say, "Nothing." The door slams shut. What follows next is a senseless conversation such as, "What do you mean, nothing's wrong? I can see something's wrong. Did somebody insult you? Did you have a fight with your friend?" All the child will say is, "I didn't have a fight with anyone." Or, alternatively, you could simply make an affirmative statement: "Something happened." There's no point in peppering the child with questions. He came home and he's out of sorts. Don' be over-curious or try to worm information out of him or try to help him. You can just sit next to him, quietly, in silence, listening with your heart. You don't always need to listen with your ears at all. Sometimes it helps to listen with other organs. There will always be time to ask questions later. Many psychologists say we should always turn the questions that are rolling around our heads into affirmative statements. For example, instead of, "Are you upset about something?" we should say, "You're upset today." However, individual relationships are important here. For example, affirmative statements don't work for my children. The children don't like them. Although I'm not fond of asking them direct questions and prefer to use the affirmative statements, I can use this approach only when my child is positively disposed. In negative situations, I have to employ direct questions, since my older son basically responds this way to the affirmative sentences: "Oh, Mom, not your psychology again! You're always sensing everything..." My younger son doesn't like the affirmatives either. His reaction is basically, "What, did you see it in my eyes again?" So, questions work better for us. Perhaps for some people affirmative statements will work better in negative situations and questions in positive. So, no one piece of advice from a psychologist can work in all cases. No one knows your children better than you. The only things that can always be effective are sensitivity and sincerity.

Concrete guidelines help a great deal when you're dealing with children. They introduce discipline and help you avoid having to continually remind, shout or punish. Children prefer concrete and very precise instructions. For example, let's say the child comes home from school and is playing. It's time to do his homework. You can tell him several times to do this. And each time the child will say, "In a little bit, I'll just finish this." After several reminders of this type, it might well happen that the parent will just blow up and the child will freak out and say something like, "Now I'm not going to do anything at all!" And then everyone's mood is ruined, both the parent's and the child's. But it's possible to approach talking with the child in a different way. When he says, "In a little bit," you can ask, "How long is that? How much more time will you need?" If the child once again says, "A little bit," then that doesn't mean you should wait some more, until that "little bit" is up. It's very hard for a child to keep track of time. An hour of playtime can fly by like five minutes. Ask him to state a specific amount of time he needs in order to finish what he's doing. For example, twenty minutes. Five minutes before that time period runs out, remind the child that in five minutes he needs to switch to doing homework. Don't allow him to extend the timeframe. In this way, the child not only learns discipline, but also begins to get better at keeping track of time.

I'd also like to include a couple of paragraphs on the topic of using pressure and inequality in your interactions with your children. It's very easy to hurt a child. Sometimes a child might not even show he's feeling hurt. Because often the reason he'll let you know is so you'll feel sorry for him. But what about if it's the person he feels closest to who's hurt him? Who will he complain to? In this case, he'll file away the hurt inside him. Fortunately, this tends to pass very quickly in children, but even so, in many cases it's possible to avoid hurting them entirely. We often speak without thinking, expressing opinions that the child can find painful, especially if he's going through adolescence. Our children hear so much criticism! Many parents place so much pressure on their children – while calling it "interacting" – that the child begins to dread every conversation with his parent because he always ends up getting the wrong end of the stick. It's good if the parent can see himself, recognize that he's angry and then, once he's let off steam, manage to go back to the child, give him a hug and ask forgiveness. What's frightening is when a parent's convinced he's in the right. Even more so when the parent knows he was wrong, that he went too far, but doesn't go make up with the child out of fear of losing his authority. That's when a wall begins to go up between the child and the parent. And with age it will only grow taller. Once the child is grown up, the wall can disappear, but it's very likely that this grown child will raise his offspring the very same way. If the wall doesn't come down by the time the child reaches adulthood, then the child might go to the other extreme: not wanting to repeat his parents' mistakes, he'll be totally permissive in raising his own child, which will also give rise to a host of relationship problems. Because while it's easy to reconcile yourself to being permissive with a little child, this becomes more and more difficult as the child gets older.

Interactions are the cornerstone of relationships. If there's no interaction, there's no relationship. Interacting in the wrong way results in the lack of a normal relationship. It leads to "problem children," "difficult children," "disobedient children", and – most important – to unhappy children. And they aren't born that way; they become that way. Often with our help.

If we observe how we interact with our children or, better yet, begin to note down the phrases we toss at our children, then before long we'll have enough material for a humor magazine. The things children say seem funny to adult ears, but imagine the little kids who have to listen to all of this. Here are some adult thoughts about the phrases they heard when they were growing up:

This is how my mom taught me to THINK ABOUT THE CONSEQUENCES: "If you fall out of that window, I won't take you shopping with me."

This is how my mom taught me to ACHIEVE THE IMPOSSIBLE: "Shut your mouth and eat your soup."

How my mom taught me to RESPECT OTHERS' WORK: "If you're intent on killing each other, then go outside. I just washed the floors."

How my mom taught me to BELIEVE IN GOD: "Pray that this stuff will come out in the wash."

How my mom taught me to THINK LOGICALLY: "Because I said so, that's why."

How my mom taught me PERSISTENCE: "You can't get up from the table until you eat the rest of that."

How my mom explained the CONNECTION BETWEEN CAUSE AND EFFECT: "If you don't stop howling, I'll slap you."

How my mom taught me NOT TO ENVY OTHERS: "Well, there are millions of the child who have worse parents than you do."

How my mom taught me to BE GROWN UP: "If you don't eat your vegetables, you'll never grow up."

How my mom taught me to FACE THE FUTURE BRAVELY: "Just you wait, I'll give you a talking to at home."

How my mom taught me the BASICS OF TAKING CARE OF MY HEALTH: "If you don't stop crossing your eyes, then they'll stay crossed for your whole life."

How my mom taught me EXTRASENSORY PERCEPTION: "Put on your sweater – I know you're cold!"

How my mom taught me the BASICS OF GENETICS: "You get that from your father!"

Adolescent Children

**The best way to make children good
is to make them happy.**
   - Oscar Wilde

The most difficult period in child raising is adolescence. If you've built your family relationships properly, then you can avoid many problems at this time. If the relationships have been ruined, then the parents will need to change first. They're the ones who will need to take the first step toward revisiting how they relate to their child, what demands they place on him, their own character. The child won't take this first step. We're older, wiser, more experienced.

What goes on with a child during adolescence? He begins to feel like an adult, but at the same time he refuses to consider the responsibilities and obligations that lead to full adulthood. He simultaneously demands more rights, but won't take on more responsibilities. The adolescent doesn't want to answer for anything at all, even with empty words. That's precisely what's so annoying for us adults about kids at this age. As far as we're concerned, our sons or daughters are still children, and nothing has changed, but for them the whole world has changed.

It's important for parents to realize at this point that whatever relationships they've built with their children during the first 13-14 years of their lives will be the key to how things will play out when he matures. If it's been an open, trusting relationship, if the parents have managed to become their child's friend, then the adolescent period will go smoothly. If the parents have thought of their child as dumb, if they've shouted at him and belittled him, then that's exactly the way the child will begin treating his parents when he gets a little older. At 13-14 years of age the child is coming into his own, gaining life's energy. Energetically he's becoming much stronger than his parents. He might still fear them on the outside, the way he used to do, but inside, he's already a volcano that's starting to wake up. He's growing strong, but at the same time he still lacks life experience and wisdom. If his relations with his parents have been unstable, then as he matures, they will only grow more strained. The child will hate his parents and do everything the opposite of how they did. If he and his parents have come to be friends, then this period will go smoothly.

Now, what happened in our family is that we found ourselves somewhat unprepared for our child's maturation. Once our second son was born, we shifted all our attention to this younger one. The older son got scolded more often, and he was given responsibility for watching his younger brother, for helping around the house, and so on. Our relationship with him grew less tender and touching. And by the time he hit age 15, we entered a period of lack of understanding. This didn't come out of the blue. Gradually, day by day, we found more and more fault with our child and were less and less patient. He started skipping school, which we, like most parents, began to address: we ordered him to do his work on time, not to miss school. We began painting an awful picture for him of the unhappy future he'd face if he didn't finish school, etc. To be honest, none of it helped. What's worse, our son's character began changing, and not for the better. He grew closed off, preferring to spend time in his room, with his headphones on, ignoring family outings and so on. We wanted to drag him out of this world he'd constructed for himself, but he wouldn't have any of it – he wouldn't even let us in! It was pointless for us to call on him to act responsibly, to order him to do anything, or to try to cheer him up or amuse him. He was all wrapped up in himself. We were being totally ignored. He paid no attention to our opinions, he considered our views on things old-fashioned, and we ourselves seemed outmoded, etc. And then we came to understand that ordering him around and placing pressure on him couldn't improve our relationship; all it could do was doom it to failure. We had to be the ones to change first, because at the end of the day, what's important wasn't for us to mold our child into some model of positive character, but to help him be happy. If the child doesn't want to go to school and wants to work instead, that's his choice. The main thing is for him to be satisfied with his life.

By the time our son turned 17, our relations had evened out. Now we spend lots of time together talking about a wide variety of topics. Sometimes he expresses worries about what career to choose, about his abilities, about finding a job. And we respond with one piece of advice: we will accept and support any choice he makes, and that the main thing is for him to be happy. You can life a happy, worry-free life while working a simple, uncomplicated job, or you can be extremely unhappy your whole life even if you have a high position. Our son began going to school, all without any pressure from our side. We gave him the opportunity to live as he wanted and to be who he wanted to be in life. He knows our support is guaranteed no matter what he undertakes to do. True, he still sometimes falls victim to the views we inflict on him because of our own inexperience. For example, he's afraid of living his life to no good end. He's afraid of not fitting in with others, of not finding a job, etc. We correct our pedagogical mistakes to the extent we can do so: we explain to him that there's no such thing as a meaningless life, that being socially awkward doesn't at all translate into not being a successful person, that it's much more important to be emotionally balanced and to have spiritual qualities than it is to be professionally marketable. We continue to work on correcting our mistakes. And we're seeing the fruits of our labor.

As a child matures, it's important to know what's going on inside him at this time. Tempests are raging there. And there's no point in causing a tempest in a teacup. It's better to wait it out. The child will issue forth categorical dismissals of everyone around him. But that doesn't at all mean that he's become callous and cruel. Don't jump to any conclusions – he'll find his way all on his own. You can gently correct him, ask him to try to avoid judging others harshly. As a general rule, all of an adolescent's character traits express themselves with heightened intensity. Attentiveness can appear right alongside callousness or even cruelty, shyness can alternate with gregariousness, greed with generosity, attention to detail and even fastidiousness with carelessness. Adolescents are usually emotionally unstable, and you can expect to see abrupt emotional mood swings, from joyful excitement to apathy and even depression. You'll get the strongest and stormiest reactions when you try to encroach on the adolescent's sense of himself. His desire for people to think well of him and recognize him can alternate with an external show of being independent, with not giving a damn, with a huge sense of pride. The desire and need to associate with adults can alternate with the desire for seclusion, to be alone. It's not a simple thing for parents to go through all of this, to witness such escapades. But hormones are at work here and you can't do anything about that. Just as in any developmental period, this one has its own specific palate of psychological reactions to the surrounding world. The adolescent's reactions can be unpredictable and have negative consequences. For this reason, the parents' help at this time is more necessary than ever before.

  If up until he's seven a child basically needs only his mother, and after seven, the child mainly needs his father, then in adolescence the child needs both parents equally as never before. But the paradox lies in the fact that both the mom and dad should act as mediating influences on the child, while also remaining in the shadows. After all, he no longer sees them as authority figures, and besides, he's no longer a child. This isn't an easy task. But it's totally doable. It's very good if someone who can serve as a mentor for the child comes into his world at this time. Neither the mother nor father can fulfill this role. We know that to be a losing equation. The child is entering the period when he's easily influenced by people he admires, and new interests are appearing. It's good if parents keep themselves abreast of all that's going on in a child's head at this point and move in step with him. But even if you manage to do this, it's still better if someone else serves as the child's mentor. It could be someone around 18-25 years of age who can become friends with the child. It can be a sports coach, or a life coach. It'll be best if it's someone the parents know and if they trust his influence on their child, since we're all aware of cases when an outside person has negatively affected a child. After all, at this age, they're very suggestible and susceptible to the influence of authority figures. Adolescents will try to imitate adults in every way. They feel like grown-ups, but for now they're still living children's lives. They still have to come home at a certain time, go to school, do their homework. So the only thing they can do is to imitate grown-ups on the surface. This is why they start smoking, have a drink, start going on picnics. They're just totally copying adults. More often than not, it ends up that their imitations come off seeming absurd, or sometimes distorted, and that their role models aren't the best. For this reason it's important that the child be surrounded in this period by people of high moral character, so that if the child emulates them, the results will be positive. Folk wisdom tells us that you become who you associate with. It works out best if the parents actively address the child's needs and seek out an authority figure to mentor him before the adolescent starts casting around for one himself. Even so, this mentor should be the child's friend, not the parents'. No adolescent will take up a friendship because his parents order him to. Closeness with a mentor will take place naturally. We got lucky in this regard: we suggested to our son that he take a capoeira class, and we weren't thinking at all about a mentor. This Brazilian martial art has its own traditions, its own rules for greeting each other. In spite of his youth, the young instructor turned out to be a very talented leader. He spent a lot of time with the kids after class, showing them various tricks, and he amazed our son with his tumbling skills. Over the course of two years, he became a genuine idol and friend for our son. He would even ask the boys to show him their report cards, and this motivated them to study. Later on, my son stopped doing capoeira, because we moved to a new city. We found an analogous capoeira school in the new place, whose coach, by the way, turned out to have been the previous coach's master. But unfortunately, the two of them didn't click. Despite his high rank, the new mentor wasn't able to draw our son in. Before long he had lost all interest in capoeira.

      Another problem that parents often encounter is that their child just looks disgraceful. Just as he changes on the purely physiological level, his tastes change, too. The little boy who just yesterday moved naturally and lightly begins to waddle, with his hands stuck deep in his pockets, hiding his head in his jacket collar or his eyes behind his cap. Girls begin enviously comparing their clothing and hairdos to those of their idols, subjecting their moms to emotional outbursts over the differences they see. I remember what a difficult time I had convincing my son not to put on two T-shirts that totally clashed with each other, and not to wear a wool cap in hot weather. The way I saw it, he looked like a matryoshka doll. The way he saw it, this outfit was cool and defiant. With my heightened aesthetic sense, I stuck to my position to the bitter end, thinking I could inculcate good taste in him. The upshot was that the adolescent period passed, and normal taste arrived on its heels. I'm satisfied by the way he dresses now, but I recall his closet at age 15 with horror. Our second son will soon reach that age, and it's a mystery what his adolescent style will be. But no matter what it is, we'll totally accept it.

One other reason for psychological difficulties in adolescence is that the child is maturing sexually. He's changing before your very eyes. Physical changes bring psychological changes along with them. The child becomes awkward and shy, gets upset over the smallest defect he finds in his body and blows it all out of proportion. His body is growing so quickly that he doesn't have time to adapt, and because of this, his movements become a little clumsy and awkward. His voice cracks and grows squeaky, and from time to time a coarse adult tone of voice breaks through. But the most visible change you'll see, and the one that confirms that the child is maturing, is in his hair. Hair miraculously begins to sprout where it's never been before. First in the pubic area, then beneath the arms, and then – hurray! – the long-awaited youthful fuzz on the upper lip and chin. Boys can't wait to finally pick up a razor and start shaving. Our son asked us to buy him a whole set of men's shaving accessories to mark this event even though, to tell the truth, there was nothing to shave. But he wanted it so badly. He rejected out of hand his father's advice to not be in such a hurry, since he'd have a whole life of shaving ahead of him – in the morning for his boss, in the evening for his wife. He had such a strong desire to try it. When, during their male heart to heart conversation, his father told him that now he'd have to shave his armpits, too, my son was flabbergasted. He promised he'd try it. Then another blow from his father stunned him even more: "You know, you'll have to start shaving your pubic area, too." To which our son replied, "Are you kidding? I hope there's no place else I'll have to shave." "No, that's the last one, and that one's really up to you," my husband replied with a laugh. And with that, we entered adult life.

We didn't have any specific conversations with him about the onset of nocturnal emissions. All we did was buy relevant books now and then, such as The Men's Encyclopedia, although of course we didn't present this to him personally; if we'd done that he wouldn't even have opened it. We'd buy these things as if we'd picked them up for ourselves and leave them in an accessible spot. There were lots of jokes on this topic and we talked a lot about marriage, also peppering our conversations with jokes. At this age, an adolescent won't accept any information directly from his parents, no matter how useful it might be. But information that pops up in the course of random conversations on this or that topic, about this or that person, when it has nothing to do with him personally – that information will definitely find its way into his brain and he'll take note of it. This is the best way to introduce something to an adolescent, since the time for scolding, edifying discussions, lectures or admonitions has long since passed. The time has come to talk with the child as you would with an adult. And this is one of the wonderful periods of child rearing. Now the two of you are on equal footing, but at the same time, you're wiser and you have something to say to the child; you have your priceless experience that you can put to use a bit here. At this stage you need to merge with him and become one whole. That way it will be much easier for him to enter adult life. Two heads are better than one, and when your hearts are also united, you can scale mountains.

As far as sex education is concerned, as I already noted, we didn't take much part in that at that point. Psychologists recommend having a special conversation with the child on this topic once a boy starts having nocturnal emissions or a girl starts menstruating. You should talk about "pestles and stamens", about the boy taking responsibility for the girl and for a possible child, and about means of contraception. It's worth taking into consideration that the age at which children become sexually active has been tending downward, and to talk about possible dysfunctions and hormonal deviations that are possible at the early stages of one's sex life. Psychologists stress that it's very important to lay a firm foundation, and you can't relieve yourself of that responsibility by shifting it to someone else. In our case, we didn't place this responsibility on anyone else, but we didn't make any special efforts in this area ourselves, either. Everything just played out naturally. We'd jokingly ask him how many children he'd like, at what age he'd like to get married, and he'd answer us jokingly, too. If something in his answers – even though he was joking – sounded an alarm for me, then I'd express a point of view that came from the Vedic teachings or scientific research. I never offered any information from myself personally! For example, in spite of the common opinion that sex is beneficial, it's not advisable to expend one's sexual energy before age 20, just as it's not advisable to put off child bearing until after age thirty, because we hit our energetic peak precisely in the period between 20 and 30. This doesn't mean that sexual energy decreases after 30. No. It's just that one's life's energy lessens. In the best case scenario, a couple who gets married after age 30 will have one child, in the worst – one, and in the very worst case, they won't even have one child, despite the fact that they may be absolutely healthy. If a couple marries before age 30, they're more than twice as likely to have three or more children, because they have a greater amount of life's energy. And energy – that's our health and our success. You can build a career after 30 just as well as you can before; the university isn't going anywhere, but your energy will trickle away. Children always provide us with an influx of new energy. And although it's totally natural for our energy to begin to fade away after 30, our children fully compensate for that. A young man between the ages of 15 and 25 is not yet capable of properly controlling his sexual energy. He's in no shape to distinguish between sexual attraction and something larger. The temptation to conquer women, to control them, is very great. That leads to expending life's energy. And although a woman is capable of becoming a good wife and mother at 18, a young man is absolutely unprepared for fatherhood. We've talked about all of this and continue to talk about it. It's possible that there is an element of sex education in this, but we don't tackle any questions about sex head on.

Although an adolescent will fight for freedom, don't forget that at the very same time he's afraid of this freedom. Psychologists who work with adolescents say that many maturing adolescents admit to wishing that their parents were stricter with them, that they would teach them what's right and wrong, what they should and shouldn't do. Sometimes total freedom can be intoxicating and an adolescent can lose his way and not know how to act. All doors are open to him, but he doesn't know which to enter. Very often they go for the closest one. That's natural, but as a general rule, the adolescent doesn't find what he's expecting behind that door. For this reason, it's a great idea to approach the most complicated doors with one's parents' help. What maturing children need most is to feel secure that they have their parents' trust and attention.

Brothers and Sisters

With the first child, the parents boil everything;
With the second, they only boil the nipples;
with the third, they just run some hot water over the nipples.
And if the dog grabs the fourth child's nipple and starts gnawing it,
then it's child's problem how to get it back!

I'm a big fan of large families. Maybe my dream of having a lot of children will come true some day. But in the meantime, I have to be content with enjoying the company of friends who've had the good fortune to be raising a lot of children. It's a real pleasure to spend time with these families. When our friends who have six children bring their whole family to visit us, it makes me laugh just to see them all crowd into the elevator. They can't even fit in! The children begin trying to figure out who should go up and who should stay and take the next trip up. It's such a pleasure to watch them. And the parents have no time to get bored. They're always surrounded by such powerful streams of energy coming from their children, that they can't help but be active, too.

Such families have very strict divisions of responsibilities. Each of them is quick on the uptake and knows what he needs to do, no reminders needed. Because each of them is placed in certain conditions in which he has to make himself comfortable. Each of them does what needs to be done in order to live in comfort. If the middle child doesn't give a toy to the younger one, then the latter will shout in his ear. If the older child doesn't put her bracelets back where they belong, the middle one will immediately snatch them, and so on. It's all very natural. In the course of taking care of one another, each of them also survives individually. On the whole, all of them do everything for each other and for themselves simultaneously. It works out very harmoniously, in an orderly fashion, and – and this is the main thing – naturally. When I observe families like these, I get the impression that the parents don't even teach the children specifically to take care of the littler ones, to help their mother, or to put everything where it belongs. The children develop these skills because other children appear in the family. Life itself teaches them all these skills. Maybe I'm wrong, and maybe there's some kind of systematic education that goes on in large families. But based on my own observations, it seems to me that this happens spontaneously. As John Wilmot said, "Before I got married, I had six child raising theories. Now I have six children and not a single theory." After all, everyone usually knows how to raise children, except for those of us who have them. In general, you could easily award mothers of several children several advanced degrees, because as a rule, they become a pediatrician, a psychologist, a career counselor, a fashion experts, and overall, a possessor of great wisdom about the questions of life. To say nothing of the main thing: the happiness they bring their children and, later, their grandchildren. This is the most genuine female happiness, and you can never have too much of it, just as you can never have too many children.

Growing up in a large family isn't easy. Children who have do so are a bit different. An abundance of children in a family means the parents approach each of them differently. Although it's common wisdom that we love all our children equally, we nonetheless treat them all entirely differently. Even when there are just two children, the parents' relationship to each will be different. But what about when there are five or six? Adler, the founder of individual psychology basically said the first child is the least fortunate, since he's like a king who's been dethroned. The birth of a second child places something like an indelible stamp on the character of the first. On the other hand, though, the good thing is that one doesn't need to worry that he'll get spoiled – all things being equal, that doesn't seem likely. When there are two children, you'll begin to see competition for the parents' attention and love. The older child will begin to try to regain his position as the sole possessor of parental attention. Of course, he'll lose. In the future he might develop leadership qualities, since he'll continue to fight for attention and try to win the recognition he didn't end up getting when he was a child. If there are only two children and they're of the same sex, then the competition between them will continue for their whole lives. It can be covert or overt. And we can see a certain paradox of life in this: while the parents are doing everything possible so their children are happy, the children themselves are doing everything possible to surpass each other. If there's only one child in the family, then he'll compete with the father for the mother's attention. He'll expect the same care and protection from everyone in his adult life that he receives from his mother when he's young. For this reason, for the most part, only children are very egotistical and they have a harder time getting along with their peers, since they didn't have to compete with anyone as children and haven't lived through that experience. The second child grows up totally focused on the first. He adjusts his pace to the first child's, and so there's nothing for him to do but run faster and faster, including in his development. The competition for attention begins, and the little one can't lag behind. For this reason, the second child always seems more developed than the first. He starts walking earlier, since the older child is always driving him on, starts talking earlier – again, so he can attract the parents' attention– and ends up being more clever, etc. A child in this situation grows up very ambitious. All his life he'll be out to prove that he's better than his brother or sister. He'll set high goals for himself, which in turn raises the risk of failure – because the higher you climb, the further you fall. The third child, if he's the last, well, you can consider him the luckiest of the bunch. He never gets knocked off his throne, but the down side is that he's a king with no power. He'll have a lot of gray cardinals around him. He'll always be surrounded by the unlimited attention of his parents and older siblings, and at the same time no one will expect anything from him – after all, he's still little. Because of this, he'll have a well-cultivated motivation to achieve something in life, to achieve something no one else in the family has achieved. There's a certain pattern to this: "I'll show them what I can do." When he grows up, this child will be very talented at what he does, if of course, he makes the right career choice. If he becomes a teacher, then he'll be one of the best; if he becomes a car mechanic, then people will say of him that he has "skillful hands." But there's another scenario that's quite possible:

the child can spend his whole life delighting in playing the role of the youngest child and not make any effort at all to grow and change. In this case, instead of becoming strong and self-reliant, he can remain dependent and helpless.

If a third child is born into this family, then the middle child usually allies himself with the older, seemingly losing himself in that child's shadow. In such cases, if the older one is into sports, then the middle child is usually interested in the humanities or music, as a kind of counterweight. Research shows that middle children are generally more sensitive to injustice and can't stand subterfuge or hypocrisy. At least they can't stand it when it's directed toward them, although they can resort to underhandedness in their relations with others. In their adult lives they continue to insist on fairness in all matters.

And parents behave differently with each of their children, too. You'll notice that they approach raising the first child more responsibly. The first child usually goes to all possible little groups in town; he's told to do well in school; and people expect him to be a high achiever, to be unique, and so on. Parents make just as much of a fuss over the second child as with the first; the only difference is that they ask less of him. When the third child is born, the parents begin to ask nothing more of the second child beyond sitting with the little one when they're gone. The parents are more experienced at taking care of a child, and thus, they're more reasonable, calmer. The mom is no longer a mother hen hovering over her chick – now she's confident, knowledgeable and decisive.

The age difference between the children also plays a significant role. If the children are born 2-3 years apart, then the model I've described above will play out in the children's relations with each other and the parents' relations with the children. If the children are born far apart, say, if there's a fifteen-year age difference between the first and last child, then the parents' approach to raising each child will be different, and as a result, the children will develop different behavior patterns. A difference in gender also plays an important role. If there are all girls and one boy in the family, then that will tell the whole story. The girls' feminine tendencies might be lessened a bit and the male tendencies exaggerated. When they grow up, these girls may find that their male side dominates in their relationships with the opposite sex, or they might downplay their feminine role, etc. This also happens in families where you have all boys and one girl. When she's grown, the girl will treat men with a bit of superiority, or be overly smug, which will in turn make it difficult for her to establish relationships with men.

All of these observations can give only a general picture of how things will turn out. Everything is so interconnected and individual that no one scientific explanation can provide a clear-cut outline or guidance. It's the parents' sensitivity and their love that help the most.

Not everyone will be able to experience having a large family. Having a lot of children is a gift of fate, a gift that may have some determining factors. The main factor is how much love the woman has in her. You can't conceive a child, bear it and give birth to it without love. I'm not talking here about artificial insemination, to which many women have to turn if they suffer from infertility. Even here you need love, because not even every couple will be able to have a "test tube baby". The natural process of conception and birth require inner readiness and a huge amount of divine energy. It is a Gift. A large family offers a unique opportunity for spiritual growth, for building up and expanding one's reserves of love, and for developing a deeper understanding of life. It's not just that the woman will fully realize her most important task – bearing children. She'll also help others realize this task's significance and help them see that it's of primary importance. I'm grateful that fate has given me the chance to have close contact with large families. Spending time in their presence, you come to understand the importance and significance of what a mother with many children is doing for all women on earth. It's hard to express this in words, but this significance is present in every conversation she has with her children, in her every act, in how she relates to every occurrence, in all that surrounds her. In families like these you can feel the love. Love for everything.

Authorship in the Child's Fate

The first half of our lives is poisoned by our parents, the second by our children. Thank goodness they at least take turns!

I would hope that this chapter's epigraph doesn't reflect your experience at all. But this is exactly the way it sometimes ends up in life. We fight with our parents, then our children fight with us and then with their own children. The mistakes we make in our relationships get passed down from generation to generation, and then we describe them using the charming phrase "generational conflict." But if you take a look at what goes on, then it's obvious that there's really no conflict there at all. This conflict exists only in our heads and is born exclusively out of the fact that we resist change. Is conflict inherent in wisdom? No. Wisdom gets along just fine with youthful pragmatism, serving as a reliable source of support and encouragement. If you combine youthful energy and adult wisdom, you can move mountains. But in practice, all of this gets stirred up together and comes out as generational conflict, and the two end up in opposition to each other. Each person insists on his right to exist, so overzealously, in fact, that he poisons the other's life. The child beings to hate his parents, then the parents begin trying to figure out how they went wrong in raising him. They can't figure out who he takes after. Instead of a affectionate team you get complete estrangement. Time is slipping away, and if the parents don't get any wiser, then they won't get another chance to make things right in the relationship until grandchildren come along. But it's easy to miss this chance, too. A child can come to hate his parents very quickly, especially in adolescence, without the parents having a clue it's even happening. Despite children's seeming maturity and affectations, they still think like children. They haven't fully inhabited adulthood yet, so when they love, they really love, and when they hate, they really hate. For this reason, the "tricks" we play on children or the mistakes we make in understanding their essence are fraught with difficulty. It's very easy for adults to lose their child's trust, respect, and love.

I'd like to focus on one of the main mistakes parents make that lead to misunderstanding and conflict. And I'll note that parents make this mistake both in regard to themselves and their children. Naturally, if we think that a certain approach works with us, we'll think it will work with our children. One of the most widespread mistakes we adults make is to encroach on our child's control over his own fate. We consider ourselves the authors of our own fate, and with this same undeniable authority, aspire to the same authorship in our child's fates. We consider it so key to participate personally in our child's fate that we fear that if we let go of the reins, the child will run wild. But in fact, he will become the person he should become, even without our participation. That doesn't mean we should stop caring for our child. Caring for children means helping them, but it definitely does not mean controlling them. Controlling means not trusting. In my book "The Path Through Unhappiness to Happiness," I wrote at length about the question of our imagined authorship over our fates. Until we let go of authorship in regard to our own fate, it's impossible for us to let go of or lessen our attachment to being the authors of our child's fate, despite the fact that this is the root of all ill will between parents and adolescents. When the child is little and helpless, it seems to us that his life depends totally on us, although even this is a big illusion. But it's a very logical illusion: the child really can't eat or drink on his own, or change his own diapers. I'll talk more about this in the chapter "Abandoned Children." But despite how logical it seems, our conviction that the child can't live without us is still illusory. In "Abandoned Children," I'll introduce several things that will prove that this is so. In every case, the child will receive precisely what he should receive in accordance with his fate, with or without your participation. Even if you're not around, he'll have everything he needs, if that is what his fate decrees. Similarly, even if you place the whole world in his hands, he'll have nothing, if the purpose for his life on earth is different. Events can develop in an incredible multitude of ways, but that's not important. What's important is that you can't live your child's life for him. You can't choose his profession for him, put all the views you consider intelligent into his head, or mold a certain kind of person out of him. Of course, there's a tendency for children to repeat their parents' life scenarios, but this happens purely because of the laws of the material world, which are just as easy to explain as the speed of light or sound. You can see the similarity between parent and child as the result of the games the adults play and the masks they don, both of which the children end up adopting, too. But these games are also "allowed" by a higher power. And so, one child will repeat his parents' patterns, while another won't or might even deviate from his parents' scenario by a full 180 degrees. Of course, psychologists have found a way to explain this. They assert, for example, that the children of alcoholics will become either alcoholics or inveterate teetotalers. But all of these theories fly out the window when you take a close look at them. Children will have exactly the kind of parents they need. Children choose their parents; they're drawn precisely to the one's who can help them gain the most from life. And here I don't mean material benefits, but rather the lessons children need in order to grow and progress. Only our false "I" needs material wealth, an easy life, convenience and comfort. Our soul doesn't need any of that. It needs to get everything from life it came to get. The soul needs to learn how to love, and it will get practice at that. Our best teachers are those closest to us, because they're the most difficult ones of all for us to love. And this is the level on which children and parents are drawn to each other: so that everyone can get the lessons they need.

We adults are convinced that we're the creators and authors not only of our own fates, but of our child's as well. As we take an active part in it, we think we're helping the child, building him, directing. But in actual fact, most of the time we're only hindering or controlling him. Parents who manage to become their child's partner are able to do this because they've weakened his authorship. There's nothing dumber than trying to mold your child into something. Children are much smarter than we are. They come into this life in order to teach us, their parents. They help us live out our life lessons, so that they become obsolete. They're *our* mentors and teachers, not the other way around. We do have something to learn from them. But that doesn't at all mean that we should tiptoe around our child and indulge his every desire. There are situations when we have to give orders or give punishment, just as there are situations when it's categorically wrong to do so. Intuition will guide our steps. But if we rely only on knowledge or psychology in our relationships with our children, then we won't have to wait long to see the consequences. Where there's knowledge, feelings are lacking, to say nothing of wisdom and intuition. Because the last two come from our heart, not from any knowledge we've read or borrowed.

Life's examples show us that a mother is more strongly connected energetically to a son, and the father to a daughter. What this means in practice, when one's interacting with children, is that the mother makes more mistakes in relation to sons, and fathers in relation to daughters. We have more troubles with the ones we love more. But that's only if we love them egotistically – although for the time being we don't know how to love any other way. Loving egotistically means demanding something in return. You can demand that people listen to you, or that they correspond to your expectations, that they behave well; you can demand status or gratitude. To love unconditionally – that's a great joy. And if we want to take the first step in that direction, we have to let go of our authorship in the child's fate. And not imagine that we're the creator of someone else's fate. After all, we sometimes don't have the strength to manage our own. There's a good exercise to help you on the path to letting go, to lessening your control over your child's fate. Imagine for a minute that you are nothing more than a cocoon or some biomaterial. You've offered up a portion of your matter to the wise natural world and have fulfilled your biological function. And imagine that your child is a decrepit elder who lived for many years before you were born – it's just that he had to exchange his flabby body yet again. He chose your cocoon for this purpose. He came out of it, so that he could move on, along his own path. You've fulfilled your purpose. Of course, you live in a different, more modern world, and there's nothing wrong with teaching this "elder" the societal conventions of behavior: you can teach him to speak correctly, to hold his spoon in his right hand and his knife in his left, but no more than that. He'll do everything else on his own. He knows what he needs to do. The main thing is not to hamper him, not to knock him off his path.

Choosing a Profession

Father: When he was your age, Napoleon was first in his class!
Son: And when he was your age, Dad, he was an emperor...

The most important and responsible moment in a child's life is when he chooses a profession. Many children already have a clear idea of what they want to do in life by the time they reach this stage. If that's the case, it's thanks to the parents' efforts. But some high school seniors still don't know who they want to be. Children who find themselves in that situation are less confident and more susceptible to stress, especially if the majority of their peers have already made up their minds. In such cases, the child will be ready to rush off in any direction at all and pick a profession, just so he won't lag behind. If his parents are constantly reproaching and criticizing him, then that will make his already difficult life worse. It will disorient him and force him to make decisions in a hurry without thinking them through. Fortunately, parents in Western society are more democratic and less demanding, so the family situation is more or less positive. Children can take a gap year after graduating from high school to relax, reflect, or travel. That helps in making a career choice. Children should also definitely spend 60-80 hours doing volunteer work. This gives adolescents the opportunity to get an accurate sense of what it would be like for them to work in this or that profession, work with mentors and try on different roles before making a decision about their future profession. These children have a wider range of choices. But the situation in Asian countries is very complex. Children there don't have the chance to test themselves through volunteer work, since that avenue hasn't been developed at all in those countries. It's not accepted to take a gap year after finishing high school. A graduate who does so will be labeled a lazybones and good-for-nothing. It's seen as something to be ashamed of, just like being held back a grade in school. Fewer demands are placed on girls, since their intended path is to tend the hearth. But young men are subjected to a great deal of pressure. Fathers sometimes demand the impossible of theirs sons, the especially in poor families. Since only those who get high scores on their government exams have the opportunity to attend post-secondary schools for free, parents often place such extreme pressure on their sons when they're preparing for these tests that suicides are not uncommon during test times. For example, last year in Kazakhstan, two students committed suicide after taking their tests. One of them left a note for his parents, in which he wrote, "Forgive me for not living up to your expectations. I've failed the test." In poor families that can't afford to pay for an education, doing well on the government tests is the only way to get into the university. For this reason, parents are fixated on drumming it into their children's heads that nothing will come of them if they fail these tests. They won't get in anywhere. Their lives will be over. These are the realities of life. All children are different, and their parents are, too, by the way. One child will fail a test and not get upset about it in the least, while another will be ready to end his life over it. And you definitely have to take all of that into account when raising a child. You can't grasp the ungraspable and you can't demand the impossible. Everything will work out just as it should. We can't live a child's life for him, and we can't determine his fate. We have no right to do so.

  We can give our child help, but if we're not sure whether we're actually helping him at a given moment or harming him, then it's better not to help him at all. A lot of times, it's more useful to ignore a problem than to stick your nose in it. Everything will work itself out: the child will find his way, maybe by making mistakes, or by trial and error, or by searching, but he'll definitely end up with a profession. What's important is to help him gain happiness, to teach him what matters in life, to help him construct the right kind of worldview, and to love life, people, and himself, and to cope with the curve balls life throws him. If the parents have taken care of what matters most – the child's life values – then all the rest will come in good time, including choosing a profession. It's these values that will help a child make the right decision at the right time.

Parents very often get into the habit of comparing their child with others. We'll often compare children without having any idea of how unpleasant this can end up being for our child, especially during adolescence, when he's trying to find a place for himself in adult life, when he's choosing a profession. It isn't our child's fault that he's not the way we would like him to be. It's our problem, and it has nothing to do with him at all. We have all kinds of desires. We all want to see our children become presidents or astronauts or scientists and so on. Sometimes dreams come true, sometimes not. But even if your child did end up embodying one of your dreams and became who you wanted him to become, there still would be no guarantee that he'd be happy.

One's childhood plays an important role in choosing a career. This is the time when it's easiest of all to get a sense of where the child's innate skills lie, the skills that will play a deciding role in his career choice. If the parents didn't pay attention to developing these innate skills and were less observant and aware of them, then those children generally have a hard time picking a profession. But if the parents watched the child and directed and helped him develop in the necessary direction from the time he was little, then he'll settle on a profession very early on and won't have any second thoughts about it. Such children are more sure of themselves, are able to set goals for themselves and pursue them. And you have the parents to thank for that.

Because they want to encourage some sort of inclination in their child, parents very often will start pressuring the child, without taking the time to figure out their child's personality type. For example, they force a future engineer to play the piano. He'd be happy to sit with a piece of cardboard and a ruler, but they force him to endure hours of boredom at the keyboard. The child isn't able to resist, and he does what he's told, although he might occasionally throw a tantrum. The parents, meanwhile, come up with an explanation for this behavior: he's just being lazy. And they think, "you have to force the child to do things, or else he won't make anything of himself." If you have the desire to sit a future physicist down with an accordion or send a musician off to swimming lessons (which won't harm their overall development) then you need to do this in a cooperative way, with both of you agreeing to it. If you don't, then it's like asking your friend to play you some music just for fun, but then handing him a pile of sheet music and saying, "I'd like some Mozart, Tchaikovsky's 'Autumn Seasons', and a little Chopin, but you can pick the rest yourself." You're implying that if he won't play what you want, then he's lazy. And maybe he will go ahead and play, but that's the last time he'll ever play for you. Children are just the same way. If you force them to do something you ask, then they'll do it out of fear and the desire to please you, and so on, but not because they're interested in doing so.

How can you determine a child's inclinations and gifts? It's easiest to do this when they're young, when their head isn't yet playing such a strong role in their actions. Kids' lives are governed mainly by their feelings and emotions, unlike adults' – adults live more through their heads and cold, hard reason. When the mind becomes active, it always seeks to benefit the person without taking into account its emotional needs. For example, mental activity might give rise to a decision to go to law school instead of becoming an artist, since lawyers earn a decent living. And the parents, who think everything through, say, "An artist isn't a real profession, it's just a hobby. You can do that in your spare time, in the evening, but have a day job and earn good money." And so the child goes to law school and spends his whole life doing something entirely opposite to his real interests. He'll become a mediocre lawyer, and if he has the time, and he's lucky, then he'll also become a mediocre artist. Because artistic talent is something you have to develop. Undeveloped, squandered artistic talents don't bring any masterpieces into the world.

You need to get a sense of a child's inclinations before he becomes as mind-oriented as an adult. What's he most drawn to? What kinds of activities bring him the most pleasure? Where does he excel? All of this shines through very clearly in childhood, but if you don't pay attention to it and develop a child in the right area, then it will be more and more difficult to pinpoint his inclinations as he gets older. If the parents don't give this aspect of childrearing adequate attention, then when he reaches adolescence, the child will end up at a giant crossroad when it comes to choosing a profession. He won't know which way to go, who to become, where to direct his energies. And there's only one way out of that dilemma – to try to find himself through trial and error.

Ancient Vedic sources describe a method for determining a child's strengths. It's totally suitable for our children. It's come down to us thanks to the deciphering and many years of research into the Vedic materials. There was a whole ritual in Hindu culture designed to revealing a child's talents, and after this ritual, the child would be educated bearing these talents and inclinations in mind. The adults would lay out several items before a child: a book, money, a hammer and a pistol. The items were laid out on the floor at a significant distance from each other, to keep the child from grabbing more than one at once. They would let the child into the room and leave him alone with the items. Then they'd watch him. A child would usually crawl first in one direction and then in another, but he'd make a choice fairly quickly and pick up one of the objects. He wouldn't know what the object was or what it was used for. The child would relate to the objects on a purely emotional level, since he wouldn't be able to determine that a pistol was for shooting, and a hammer for working in a workshop. Nonetheless, he'd make his choice based on the feelings he experienced, subconsciously, intuitively. He'd choose what he liked most, what was most visually appealing to him, what seemed most pleasing to him. If you repeat this this experiment some time later, the child will pick the same object the second and third times. For example, if a child chooses money, then it's likely that he bears within him the seeds of a future financier. Here the parents should develop an interest in economics, finance and math. If he chooses a book, then he tends more to theoretical knowledge. He might well become a scientist or a researcher. If the child is drawn to the hammer, it means he's more interested in physical labor. He'll enjoy constructing something, working with his hands, i.e., he'll get more satisfaction from physical labor than intellectual work. If the child chooses the pistol, then he likes to wage war, preserve his rights, and lead. He might become a good strategist, soldier or a talented military commander. After carrying out this testing, the parents continue to observe their child. For example, they look to see what the child's more drawn to when he's playing: to building blocks or books, or whether he prefers playing in the sand box to singing and dancing, or whether he likes to mold something out of clay instead of running around the gym, and so on. These observations are very valuable. They help the parents orient the child, steer his development in the necessary direction, and sharpen the traits he'll need for each skill.

Each person has talents and capabilities. There are no untalented people. But there are a great many people who haven't discovered their talents and capacities. It's the parents' job to help the child do this. As the wise men tell us: we have two hands and we can't grow a third. But parents often don't pay attention to what the child already has, and instead try to mold something more out of the child, develop something unnecessary – they try to grow a third hand. They can spend a lot of effort and energy on this, but in the end nothing will come of it. The child will grow up and won't ever sit down at a piano again, or dance, and the reason is that when he was little, his parents tried to make him into a dancer, etc. Really, the Vedas tell us that four things are inlaid in a person's fate long before he's even conceived: how long he'll live, his talents (or profession), the extent of his wealth, and the time of his death. So, a child will become who he's meant to become. But whether he'll find his path easily or not, that depends on his parents.

You definitely can't go wrong or make a mistake if you strive to develop the kind of general qualities that are necessary and common to any profession. These include honesty, generosity, unselfishness, the ability to help others, and compassion. But in order to inculcate these traits in a child, the parents themselves must possess them fully and completely. What's important is not to give a child an amazing school education, but to help him, first of all, to become a Person, and second of all to become a happy person. And only after that, third, comes being a highly skilled specialist. Because if a person tends toward working in business and his parents notice this gift in him in a timely fashion and do all they can to get him the appropriate education, but don't take care to develop honesty or generosity and don't teach him to be upstanding, then it's not inconceivable that he'll become a super successful businessman and make a good career for himself, but that at the same time his soul will suffer incommensurately. If greed, vanity and egoism dominate in his professional life, then his career will have a sad end. That's not the way for a person to be happy.

The Incomplete Family

**The best possible mother is the one
who can take the father's place when he dies.
 – I. Goethe**

According to statistical research, the United States is first in the world in terms of number of divorces (4.95 per 1,000 people.) Puerto Rico comes in second (4.47 per 1,000 people,) and Russia is in third place. Canada comes in eighth, with 2.46 divorces per 1,000 people. According to Canadian Divorce Statistics, the number of divorces peaked in 1987 in connection with the introduction of a new divorce law. In recent years, this number has begun to fall. However, Statistics Canada states: "About 38 percent of all marriages taking place in 2004 will have ended in divorce by 2035. For married families with children, 18.6 percent of children live with only one parent. Common-law families are growing faster than any other type of family, with one in ten Canadians living in such relationships and 14.6 percent of children living with common-law parents." As research by the Vanier Institute of the Family in Ottawa shows, "most children of divorce experience some level of distress, which often lasts for over a decade." The study says, "For instance, they miss the other parent and, when little, they may feel that they are partly to blame for the divorce; some desperately try to get their parents together again; they are sad; some cry a lot, while others lash out and develop behavioral problems."

The number of divorces clearly indicates how many children are being raised in incomplete families. While families headed by mothers are the most numerous, the number of families in which fathers are raising children on their own is growing. There's no doubt that an incomplete family affects a child's emotional state. And although the reasons incomplete families occur are varied and individual – these can include widowhood, or divorce, or children being born out of wedlock – parents face pretty much the same difficulties. Even so, statistics once again show that in families where the child is being raised by one parent as the result of the death of the other, his upbringing tends to turn out more positively than in families that are incomplete as a result of divorce or single motherhood. This is partly explained by the fact that grief unites the surviving relatives, and the child doesn't feel deprived in terms of contact with grandparents and so on. Empathy and compassion dominate in such families, rather than bitterness and hurt. You'll find the most positive outcome in families with siblings. In these families, the older child intuitively takes the younger one under his wing. The younger child feels watched over and protected. The children help each other, and there's much less competition between them. They don't feel they're not getting enough attention, or feel lonely or inferior.

The situation for an only child in an incomplete family is more complicated. The mothers usually feel sorry for their children and want to give them everything and more! They try to compensate for the lack of paternal attention with material things. In spite of any financial difficulties the family might be experiencing, the children, as a rule, are the best dressed, and they have the most toys and the most expensive cell phones. The mothers often skimp on themselves, even depriving themselves of necessities, so they can give their children absolutely everything. Most children who grow up in such families end up very egotistical. And egotism is a direct path to suffering in adult life. The danger of raising an egotistical child is greater if he's the same gender as the parent. For example, in such families, the mother isn't able to recognize that her child is becoming egotistical. The mother will be deeply offended by the slightest hint that this is the case. She denies what's before her very eyes, and she'll defend her childrearing approach to the very end, since she can't imagine her relationship with her child being any other way. One day I had occasion to do a consultation with a family with a single mother and a daughter. The daughter was becoming very demanding and spoiled. At about age 12, the daughter began experiencing nosebleeds and fainting spells, which happens quite often with children who are used to getting excessive attention from their parents. They ran tests on the girl at the hospital, but couldn't find any cause of the fainting and nosebleeds. All the tests came back within normal ranges. The mother was perplexed. She immediately rejected out of hand the possibility that her daughter was fainting because she didn't want to accept her circumstances. I've observed that it's not always easy to discern that the desire for everything to be just the way she wants it to be has penetrated deeply into a child's subconscious. She might not throw tantrums, and on the outside she might do what she's asked to do and might even submit to your wishes, but deep inside she'll protest and be ill at ease. The child doesn't faint on purpose because she doesn't like something. But her body does that for her. It simply shuts down because it's incapable of and unwilling to accept things as they are. The body has an easier time losing consciousness for a couple of minutes. Egoism is so great that it doesn't entertain the option of seeking solutions or a way out. It's my way or no way at all. Now, that doesn't mean that the child will faint as soon as he experiences some kind of external irritation. That process can extend out in time. After all, this idea that "everything has to be the way I want it to be" doesn't take root in the subconscious in just one day. It takes years of misguided upbringing to accomplish that. Similarly, the body needs time to process the external irritation and respond with a fainting spell. For this reason, it's a bit difficult to trace this connection back, but it's there. All the mother needs to do is to adjust her approach to interacting with her child, and the fainting will stop.

Another problem you see in the way single mothers raise their daughters is that they teach them a misguided approach to their relationships with men. For example, mothers risk raising an egotistical daughter who has an incorrect, distorted view of her relationships with the opposite sex and who has a difficult time imagining that a man could even be desirable. For this reason, daughters often end up repeating their mothers' fate: it's difficult for them to build relationships with men and, consequently, to build a family. Single fathers run the risk of raising egotistical sons who subconsciously dislike women.

You'll see the other extreme in single parents with children of the opposite sex. For example, mothers, terrified of losing control over their sons, are often unreasonably strict with them during the adolescent years. They're afraid the son will fall in with bad company, or start smoking and so on. And if that happens, there won't be any firm paternal hand or male shoulder to rely on. Although experience shows that if a child is drawn to hang out in bad company because that's the way his worldview has already taken shape, then no male hand will be able to pull him out of it. You need to employ other methods and approaches if this happens, ones that don't use force or cruelty at all. When mothers are strict with their sons for no good reason, they often don't think about how the child will react to this. She can't take the father's place – children understand and react differently to their mothers' and fathers' remarks. If a father corrects him, then the child sees it as simply a correction, but if the mother is critical, then boys understand that as "she doesn't love me," which has profoundly negative consequences, especially during adolescence: either the child will begin to offer more resistance – literally to everything the mother says – or if the mother is strong-willed and cruel and powerful, then he'll turn into an infantilized mama's boy, a role he'll continue to play out in his adult life as well. Sometimes you'll see a pair like that when you're walking along the street: an old mother with a cane in one hand and with her son on her other arm. They're generally always together, and live together until they die. If the son does get married, then he'll quickly get divorced, since he won't value his spouse. Since he's been brought up wrong, he developed his own idiosyncratic approach to the opposite sex, and he'll carry this model with him throughout his life. When single fathers raise girls, although there are difficulties, they aren't as numerous, mainly because of the more rational male approach to solving problems. In their very makeup, men are more spiritual, while women are more physical beings. It's been that way since time immemorial. Together these two form a flawless pair. When they come together properly, when a woman finds the right man and the man finds the right woman, the spiritual unites with the physical, and the two transform into an endless stream of energy. But separately, women generally display physicality, with a veneer of spirituality, while in men what comes out is spirituality layered over with a steadfast physicality. Male spirituality doesn't manifest as prominently as female physicality, but even so, it is extremely significant.

    I've never understood why wives complain about their husbands, saying that their children's upbringing lacks the necessary male influence. The simple fact of the father's presence in the home every day, even if he just lies dully on the couch with the newspaper, is sufficient to bring the necessary element of paternal influence to bear on the childrearing. Physically materialistic mothers, for whom nothing is ever enough and who want as much as possible and want it immediately, make the common and basic mistake of not valuing this element. So, when a single father is raising a child on his own, then as paradoxical as it might seem, childrearing problems arise less than they do with single mothers. It's possible that children don't receive enough tenderness and physical affection from their fathers, but they always get the right amount of good sense, patience and decency. Fathers don't try to play a mother's role, but mothers very often try to play the role of the father. They try to be both a mother and a father to their children. If a woman decides to remarry, then her main priority will be finding a father for her child rather than a life partner for herself, which is yet another mistake she makes. That's because it's only once a man has fallen in love with a woman that he is capable of loving and accepting her child, not the other way around. For this reason, it makes more sense for the woman to focus on her love for the man and on his feelings for her, and not on how he feels about her child. Even a child's own father will often admit that when he's away from the family, he misses his wife more than he does his children. Why does this happen? Because in life, a man "runs" energetically off his wife's energy. She's like a motor for him, just as a woman is energetically connected to her children. One can disagree about this topic, but the fact remains, that no matter what stories a childless woman might make up about how self-sufficient and satisfied she is with her life, if she doesn't have children she will all the same remain unfulfilled and energetically obstructed. Men are also affected: no matter how marvelous his bachelor life might seem to him, on the deepest level a man will still always search for a woman.

    Speaking about childrearing in incomplete families, Benjamin Spock said, "The mother's task is not to attempt to replace the father, but rather, to create an atmosphere in which the child can create an image of the father in his own imagination." Children think in images, and adults do, too, by the way. Even if a child has never laid eyes on his father and hasn't ever heard about him, he'll still have some kind of image of him in his head, one he's formed from bits and pieces of impressions of various people. He'll carry that image with him throughout his entire childhood. If the mother injects the child with some negative image of his father, then that's what he'll bear with him. For this reason, it's very important to give the child the opportunity to possess a father, if only in his imagination. Wise mothers don't create a specifically positive or negative image of the father. They simply give the child the chance to spend as much time as possible with his father. It doesn't matter how well the parents get along. This should not affect the child's interaction with the father. The situation becomes more complicated if the father is entirely out of the picture. If this is the case, then once again, the child has every right to his own image, even in his imagination. The mother can help the child create this image. She shouldn't add anything negative to it, because any negative impression of the father is simply the mother's personal impression of him. The child has an entirely different impression. She shouldn't impose labels or force a specific image of his father on him, no matter how accurate and true that image might be, because all of that is no more than the mother's personal evaluation of reality. The mother should grant her child the right of creating his own picture of his father, grant him the right to memories of him.

    A parent who's raising a child alone doesn't need to be a victim of circumstances, some kind of martyr who's suffering the fate of bringing up a child on his or her own. When parents get caught up in their emotional worries, without even realizing it, they distance themselves from their children, who at the best of times find it difficult to witness their parent's bitterness and suffering. The child begins to project the situation onto himself and blame his mother's or father's problems on himself. Of course, suffering can bring people together and form a bond between them just as love can do, but in this case, there's no point in wallowing in one's own suffering and causing the child more pain in the process. Time will pass, but the image of his mother or father that has been stored within the child during this period of suffering, divorce and pain, will remain. For this reason it makes sense to limit the extent to which you honestly share your emotions at certain times. The ideal way to approach childrearing in an incomplete family is to include relatives in the process. Unfortunately, divorced women only rarely keep up good relationships with their in-laws. In order to achieve this, you need both love and wisdom. If you've managed to maintain good relations with the relatives, then a child's interactions with them will partially compensate for the lack of one parent. If you haven't been able to do this, then, whether you're a mother or a father, you've got a Herculean task ahead of you in terms of helping the child assimilate the behavioral skills appropriate for his or her gender.

Abandoned Children

**We bear children with ease and without the slightest worry,
but we give so little thought to creating a person!
- Maksim Gorky**

I had the opportunity to spend several years working in a shelter for abandoned children. So, I couldn't *not* write a chapter about children who are being raised by strangers in state institutions. It also seemed right to include this chapter because this experience I've had working with orphans might possibly help parents take another look at how they're raising their own children.

Children in shelters are a special topic. These children are entirely different from children being raised at home. Abandoned children have a different mentality. These are smart, open, well-developed, but deeply unhappy children. As they grow, their feeling of hurt creeps deeper and deeper within them. You no longer see it on the surface, but the child turns into a taker. If a child has grown up in an orphanage, then when he's grown, he'll think the world owes him. Orphans feel that everyone owes them, all the time. They've grown accustomed to feeling sorry for themselves, and they'll spend their whole lives feeling sorry for themselves, either openly or in secret. When they grow up, they're capable of adapting to life in society, making a career for themselves and becoming quite successful, but their issue of feeling that no one needs them will haunt them their whole lives. In their adult lives, these people become exceedingly strident, pushy, and even rude. Because they think everyone owes them. But that is just a mask, beneath which hides their complex of feeling unneeded.

    If children in an orphanage find a family by the time they reach the ages of 10-13, then their character changes, and they have an easier time. The child will adapt to his new family easily, if the parents want him to. During my years working as an adoption coordinator in an orphanage, I saw only two instances of families giving children back to the orphanage because the relationship hadn't worked out. The parents complained that the child was withdrawn. But the social worker knew that it was the parents who didn't want to work on making the relationship fall into place – it was the parents who ended up not being ready for the child. The child is always ready. He'll adapt to any circumstances – after all, the desire to receive love and tenderness and care are part of human nature. The two cases in which the parents returned the child were with local families. And it was good that they gave the children back. It represents a double betrayal for the child, but better to live through that in childhood, than to suffer with parents like that your whole life. Not a single family I worked with on an international adoption has ever returned a child. And not because it was too far to travel, but because families who go through international adoptions are generally more prepared to adopt than local families. One explanation for this is that adopting internationally is a long process. Another is that these families were unable to become parents in their own country. When foreigners adopt, their desire comes more out of their own suffering. It's had time to ripen and is more strongly motivated. For them this is their only chance. They spend years getting the paperwork together, waiting in line for a child; they want a child. Families who go through local adoptions tend to approach the process more lightly, and less responsibly. All doors are open to them, so they often rush into a decision.

Children prepare for their meetings with adoptive parents with such hope! The adoption process is less emotional with one-year-olds. The parents acquaint themselves with the child's medical history, pick him up, and immediately fall in love with him (or don't fall in love with him and ask us to bring them a different child.) Everything is more complicated when the children are older. They immediately understand that a future mother and father are there and that they'll pick one child. The children try to be liked with all their might. The little girls put on their best dress and put ribbons in their hair, and the little boys put on their best little suits. The children aren't told that people have come to pick out one of them. They're told that the orphanage will have guests that day. But the kids all get what's going on. They understand that only one of them will be chosen, and that that one child will be sent to live with a family. The children vie with each other to recite poetry, sing songs and show how good they are at counting and writing. There are also shy children, who keep off to the side. They also want to be liked, but they don't know how to make this happen. This is always very emotionally difficult for the parents – it's hard to decide on just one child. There have been cases when the adoptive parents, especially Americans, once they've seen the available children, have requested that the embassy grant them permission to bring two adopted children into the country at once, even though they'd originally intended to adopt only one.

Hundreds of abandoned children have found families in the United States, Spain, Belgium, France and Great Britain. Over the course of seven years, I worked directly with adoptive families from all of these countries. The children have already grown up and become like native-born children in their countries and families. Every year my e-mail inbox is full to bursting with photos of the happy families. The parents still send me reports about their children, their successes and achievements. They've managed to bring happiness to both the children and themselves. Of course, there have been tragic cases related to adopted children in the United States. There are cases of bullying and murder. But this isn't connected to where the child is living. The same thing can happen to children in their biological families. Fortunately, all of my clients became successful parents. All of the adoptive parents I've worked with have become loving, caring mothers and fathers. And the fact that their children have grown up happy is a testament to that fact.

Sometimes parental love knows no bounds. Everyone knows this and understands it. However, we often underestimate a child's love. It's only been through working in an orphanage that I've come to understand what a deep and unconditional love a child can have for his mother.

Here's an example from real life. The mother of an eight-year-old boy was an alcoholic and was leading a dissolute life. There were always many various men in their small apartment. The mother would drive the child out into the freezing weather so that he wouldn't bother her. She'd force him to go begging. The boy would then bring home whatever money he'd managed to collect on the streets. The mother would use this to money to treat her drinking buddies. If he came home empty-handed, she'd beat him. A social worker found out what was going on and had the boy placed in an orphanage, and the mother was deprived of her parental rights. The boy was now living in a warm spot, under good conditions. He began to make friends. This orphanage, our orphanage, was one of the best in the country. Even so, the boy would run away any chance he got. He'd walk several kilometers along the highway in the freezing cold just to get home. Then he'd explain to us that he couldn't bear being away from his mother, that he was worried about her, that he was afraid she wouldn't make it without him – who else other than him would bring her something to eat? And there are hundreds of cases just like this one. No matter how bad the mother might be, to her child she's still the best mother there could possibly be. Maybe she cast him aside and doesn't even remember he exists, but he'll still love her and wait for her his whole life, and when he grows up, he'll go looking for her. It often happened that mothers would abandon their child right on the orphanage's doorstep. For whatever reason, they couldn't bring themselves to come inside and sign papers to give the baby up. If the mother signs this form, then the child stands a chance of being adopted, but without it, he'll be classified as abandoned. And that means he'll be in the orphanage for a long time. By law, the mother has six months to change her mind, come back, and claim the baby. Once this period elapses, the police and social workers begin looking for the mother. If they don't succeed, then the child receives a new name (usually the name of the employee who found the baby) and a new birth certificate with an approximate birth date. The children whose mothers thought to include their birth certificates inside their blankets are the lucky ones. There have been cases in which the mother was found, but when she was asked to sign the forms to officially give up the baby for adoption, she had no real idea what was being asked of her and couldn't even remember his date of birth.

One of the factors leading to overflowing orphanages in Muslim countries is shame. It's not accepted to give birth there if you're not married. Inexperienced young women who come to the large cities to go to school often fall victim to experienced Don Juans. Because the girl is sexually inexperienced, she often realizes she's pregnant only some time later. She can't admit it to her parents, because that would bring shame to the family. The only way out is to have the baby and give it up for adoption. Fortunately for them, the academic year lasts a whole year, and by the time she goes back to her home village, no one will have to know anything. The majority of children in orphanages in Kazakhstan has been left there by young women. They never come back for them. They get married and start a new life. The husband will never find out that the wife has a child. Of course, sometimes the wife does feel remorseful and comes to claim her child. This often happens right at the moment when the child is about to be put up for adoption. It's as if the birth mother senses that this is her last chance to see her baby. In such cases, the adoptive parents fade into the background. Naturally, this is stressful for them – they've grown attached to the baby and already consider him theirs, and suddenly the mother comes on the scene. But she has every right to do so. Were she to come back later, after the judge's decision was legally binding, then the adoptive parents' rights would prevail. They're protected in these cases by the law regarding anonymous adoption. But until the judge's ruling takes effect, the mother has every right to decide the fate of the child, even if he's being raised by the government.

The next group of women who give up their babies are city women living dissipated lives. They have a baby and give him up. Then a year later they have another baby, this time with a different father, and they give that one up, too. The smallest group of children is made up of those whose parents are ill or deceased.

Why do I mention all of this? It's all connected to the topic of the child's personal control over his own fate. Parents lay excessive claim to the right to control their children's fate. In actual fact, the child will receive what fate has in store for him, no matter what. Even if his mother abandons him, in the freezing cold, leaving him to die defenseless and helpless, the child still will not die if he's fated to live. If he's fated to have all the best in life, then he will definitely have that. He can be chosen by the best possible parents in the world and be the beneficiary of all possible worldly benefits. But the opposite can also happen. One can watch over a child with an eagle eye and shelter him, but then let your guard down at a pivotal moment, and disaster strikes.

It seems to us that a little child is utterly defenseless and couldn't survive without us. But while a child is little and can't take care of himself, he's under greater protection by God than by any grown-up. We have freedom of choice, but children don't. For this reason they have more unseen defenses than we have. For example, take the fact that recently stunned the worldwide press: a child who was at one point left in an orphanage in Kazakhstan, wanted by no one and forgotten by everyone, last year inherited a multi-billion dollar pharmaceutical company in the United States. True, the child's American adoptive mother died suddenly. If it's someone's fate to grow up without parents, then he'll grow up without them. If the child is fated to grow up in a family, he'll acquire a family, if he's spent his early years in an orphanage. Very little depends on us. Parents are nothing more than cocoons. Their task is to give a child life and teach him the most elementary rules of behaving in society, rules that will help the child survive. But if they take on a larger role than they should, then problems will arise, not only in the parents' relationships with their children, but also in the children's fate. I always encourage parents to loosen their control, believe in the child and in his strengths and abilities. Everything he needs will come, without fail and break through. The main thing for us is not to hinder the process.

Blind Love
Blind love has a blind guide.
- **Zulnora**

Of course, we all love our children. We want only the best for them. We correct their behavior with only the best of motives. We want the child to grow up "right" and be a successful person. We want him to have a good profession and make a good living. That is every parent's dream. In the large scheme of things, what lies beneath all these desires is that we want one thing: for our child to be happy. But who ever said that he can't be happy without a good education or career or a job? Who thought that one up? On the contrary, if you set these kinds of goals for a child and program him for success, but fate ends up surprising him with an entirely different result, then the child will end up very unhappy. And fate can deal any hand at all. Anything can happen in life. The parent's job is to teach the child to be happy no matter what the external circumstances, no matter how his life turns out or what course it takes. The parent's job is to teach the child to love life in all its manifestations. If you can't do that, then it's better not to teach the child anything at all, because if you nudge a growing carrot in this or that direction, then the carrot will quickly turn from being strong and straight into being crooked and useless. And parents will often pull their growing "carrot" in a variety of directions: the father pulls in one direction, the mother in another. The carrot itself is no idiot. It knows what it needs. It's drawn toward the light, toward the sun. But people get in its way. You end up with a crooked carrot, and then the parents ask, "How did my child turn out this way?"

We ourselves at one point allowed this unforgivable parental "love" and sheltering to creep into our relationship with our older son. Fortunately, we came to our senses in time, before our "carrot" grew crooked. Now the most we do is to "fertilize" him a bit. We realized our mistake quite unexpectedly. When my son was 15, I noticed that he'd become sadder than I'd expect him to be at his age. He had no energy and he was unhappy, even though he had his whole life before him – after all, this is the age for living the carefree life of Riley. But not for him: his head was full of gloomy thoughts. In the course of our conversations with him, it came out that our child was worried about what he'd end up being in life. About whether he'd be successful. Whether he'd find a career for himself and find a job. He began asking us questions: but what if he didn't get into any college? Could he work in his father's company? You have to have stuffed a child's head so full of useless ideology in order to turn him into a 15-year old being who's thinking and worrying about the future, who's suffering. But we ourselves turned him into that. We were constantly hovering around him, pointing him in the "right" direction, correcting his course. As a result, at age 15 the child no longer felt any lightness in his life. He'd built up too many different "you have to's" in his head. And it was all the fault of our desire to mold him into something, the fault of our fear that we wouldn't raise him correctly. Think about it – a person can deal with criticism from anyone at all, even from the whole rest of the world, but he can't cope with criticism from his parents. But we forget that point and cause our child many painful moments, all the while calling it by the beautiful name of "upbringing." Fortunately, we understood this in time and began working to repair the mistakes, which were primarily ours. I've written about these mistakes in detail in my book *The Path Through Unhappiness to Happiness.*

It's our job to teach a child to be happy. But unfortunately, that's an impossible job unless we parents ourselves learn to do this. We can't give our children something we don't possess ourselves. None of the world's riches and no success can replace a state of peace, tenderness, and feeling satisfied with oneself. Enjoying life, whether you possess the bare necessities or not even the bare necessities – that is an art. And only when we ourselves have mastered this art can we pass it on to our children. Everything else is nothing more than aimless wandering through life in search of material or sensual pleasure. But these are fleeting, and once he's deprived of them, a person is once again unhappy.

Blind love is one of the factors that prevents us from being happy and from making our children happy. It is essentially egotistical. So egotistical that, for example, many parents might love their children, but at the same time feel hatred toward others' children. Is such a thing really possible? My interactions with various parents have shown that in fact, it is. They love only their own children, because that is their own little circle: in other words, they love themselves as reflected in their children. Although if you dig a little deeper, you'll find that such parents really don't truly even love themselves. They merely nag their children to love them, leading life with a barter mentality: right now I'm giving you all my attention, and when I'm old, you'll give me yours. Of course, many people don't even realize they're doing this.

Blind parental love can prevent a child from working his way through certain moments in childhood that he'll certainly encounter in adult life as well. And as a result, the child will end up not be prepared for that adult life. When we shelter our children excessively, we deprive them of the chance to develop freely, to experiment, to test the reliability of their world. We disturb the flawless and free development that is their birthright. This leads them to keep their feeling sin, and blockages, childhood traumas and issues build up inside them. As a result, as grownups they're saddled with a full array of psychological problems. And it's unlikely that it would occur anyone to think that it's all because of blind parental love.

Maternal love is particularly dangerous. The mother has more influence on the child's fate than the father, which is explained by the mother's closer connection with the child. For this reason, the mother has a great responsibility to express her love in appropriate doses. I use the phrase "doses" deliberately, a word that might seem out of place when you're talking about love: after all, we don't need to limit out love or measure it out, and you can never have too much of it. But it's *true* love that can never be excessive, unconditional love, which is always wise, which always goes hand in hand with reason. But here I'm talking about the blind, egotistical, unconscious love that you find in most mothers. For example, if a mother's love for her son is blind and unreasonable, then that can affect his fate in life. It will be difficult for him to choose a mate and come out from under his mother's influence. The same thing can happen with daughters, too. The daughter is all the mother has, and so she receives a massive dose of "love."

Blind parental love prevents the child from investigating the world on his own. When the child is investigating the physical world, we protect him from boiling water, fire, heights, and we do this instinctively, thereby transferring our survival instinct to our child. But what are we doing when we try to protect our child from expressing his feelings? We're deforming him, and all in the name of love. In childhood, a child experiences all the same situations he'll encounter later on in his grownup life. He experiences them in a child's way. He might feel sadness, boredom, envy, anger or fear. But often the parents don't allow the child to fully experience all of this, don't give him the chance to fully be present in these emotions. "It's not good to envy people." "Little boys shouldn't cry." "There's nothing to be afraid of." With our "this is right" and "this is wrong" we don't allow our children to fully immerse himself in the world of feelings and to work through all of this during childhood. As he grows up, he'll begin to be shy about showing his true essence. This kind of person will be fully controlled by his calculating mind, which will immediately take control of every situation. Boredom that has been repressed in childhood can easily transform and grow into chronic sadness, anger can grow into cruelty, and envy into grasping, jealousy and greed. We need to accompany our child through all these childhood situations. Accompanying him means granting these emotions' right to exist, noticing them, becoming friends with them, and not attempting to immediately root out the child's boredom by offering some new form of entertainment. When he displays emotions that they consider negative, protective parents immediately take things into their own hands and don't give the child any chance to take steps on his own. Maybe the child is bored and has nothing to play with, so we say we'll definitely go to the store the next day and buy him a new toy. Or if the child is in a bad mood, we say, "Now, now, quiet down, you can't yell like that, you'll scare the neighbors." When the child expresses anger, it's important to explain to him that his reaction is totally normal, that it's a reaction to something he doesn't like. To explain to him that the main thing is not to hurt other people when expressing his anger. That's his reaction, it arises inside him and is in no way connected with anyone outside him, despite the fact that it seems that it's everything around him that's at fault. As he gets a little more mature, the child will develop a healthy relationship to anger – both others' and his own. Such people generally easily let go of anger, because they've worked through it in childhood.

Blind parental love and over protectiveness don't give the child the chance to fully experience his feelings. One time our younger son started complaining that he was bored: "Mom, I'm bored, I don't have anything to do." Maybe all children say this to their mothers. And when they do, they're looking for either attention or entertainment. When this would happen, I'd set everything aside and sit down with my son in a quiet spot, and we'd take a look at that boredom. We'd experience the boredom together. This worked like a charm. In a little while, the boredom was gone, as if someone had plucked it away with their hand. Now that my son is older, when I ask him whether he's every bored at home, he replies, "How can you be bored at home? I might be bored somewhere else, but at home there's always something I can do, especially when I don't have school." I'm happy that he's no longer a knight without a quest. Children who are allowed to experience boredom when they're little usually only rarely feel bored as adults, and if they do feel bored, they usually pass out of that state pretty quickly.

In contrast to our older son, whom we took such pains to shower with parental love, as parents always do with their first born, the younger one is growing up more open, sociable, jolly and, as a result, happier. That's because we didn't make the same mistakes with him that we made in raising our older son. Because we were young and inexperienced, our older son received the maximum possible sheltering and attention from us. And as a result, he exhibits less self-sufficiency in his adult life.

So, parents should exercise caution when it comes to showing their love and fussing over their child. This kind of excessive fussing can have unexpected negative consequences.

Parents often say that it's easier to raise someone else's children than one's own. We usually don't have problems dealing with others' children: they grow up smart and capable, while our own kids may not blossom in the way the parents would like. This can happen even if the children grow up in the same family. This happens because one doesn't experience blind love toward other people's children. Their guardians love them, of course, but they're most focused on meeting the child's basic needs. But with our own children, we go overboard: we confuse wants, whims and feelings with needs. Parental love is in full force, and of course we have nothing but the best intentions, so common sense falls by the wayside.

A Gender Neutral Upbringing

**Nothing that seems like an innovation
can be genuine.
What's genuine is always present within us.
– Maharshi**

Another amusing topic related to upbringing is gender difference. I'm not going to spend a long time on this topic, since I don't have much experience with this area. I've raised boys, and I have no idea how difficult it is to raise girls. But I'd like to focus on the question of "gender-neutral" upbringing, which is gradually becoming more fashionable in the West. Fortunately, I don't have any experience in this arena, either, because I wouldn't under any circumstances think of experimenting on my children in such a radical way. I think that people from eastern cultures, from the Caucasus, people who from an early age instill in their daughters the idea that they'll be mothers, and teach their boys that they will be the main providers, will never comprehend or adopt the West's views on this question. Only Western freedom and free-thinking could drive people to this kind of experimentation.

Not so very long ago, Western society literally exploded. Everyone was caught up in lively discussion of a Canadian family's decision to raise their child without divulging his gender:

An unconventional couple in Canada announced that they are keeping the gender of their child a secret. The couple says that they don't want their baby to be limited by the gender expectations placed on him/her by society. They want the baby to be free to play with whatever toys he/she wants to and wear whatever outfits that he/she wants to. Even the grandparents are unaware of the gender of child. The baby's siblings are sworn to secrecy and the parents have also stated that they are in no hurry to inform the child itself of which gender it is. They hope baby will come to his/her own conclusions about which gender he/she best identifies with. The baby also has 2 older brothers, five and two years old. The parents have tried to also raise them in an environment uninhibited by gender stereotypes. The oldest brothers like to wear their hair in long pigtail braids. This story is taking the media by storm. Many reports have been done, and the case has been mentioned on multiple news networks. As a survey has shown, 11% of respondents supported the parents' idea. They found it to be a great idea, while 89% thought it was a terrible idea. The couple has been bombarded with criticism, but stands by their decision. The child's mother is quoted as saying, "The idea that the whole world must know our baby's sex strikes me as unhealthy and voyeuristic."

Another Canadian couple began a similar experiment on their children two years before this current story. They employed a similar strategy nearly two decades ago. As the parents say, today their "children have turned out just fine." They had their first child in 1992 and a second three years later. The children's birth announcements intentionally omitted the sex – both are girls and were born at Ontario's

Kitchener-Waterloo Hospital – as part of an ongoing strategy to prevent gender bias from entering their children's lives. The father said the effect of his family's decision was felt most by the parents, not the children. "This had no significant effect on the children or on their interactions with others," the father told Postmedia News. "It had a significant effect on us, their parents, and a mostly short-term effect on our interactions with other adults," he said.

And very recently, yet another Canadian couple adopted the idea of raising their children in a gender neutral way. The ranks of creative parents are filling up with ever more innovative experimenters. But you don't need to worry about the children who are subjected to these kinds of experiments. Luckily, wise Mother Nature has provided for every eventuality, even when people raise their children without gender. Nature is strong and wise and will always take everything into account: in every case, a little girl become an adolescent girl and then a woman, and a little boy will become an adolescent boy and then a man. Of course, there's the danger of some destabilization in the behavior of these children in society. But if you bear in mind that children have a strong impulse to imitate others, then either boys or girls who have been raised in a gender neutral way will soon begin to behave in society as their nature dictates. Thus, all we can do is laugh at parents who raise their children this way. Give it your best shot, just try – maybe you'll be able to outsmart nature. If the goal of these experiments is to change society, to force us to treat everyone the same, regardless of their gender, then that's a different question. But in this case, I wouldn't place my children on the altar of any idea, even the most noble idea in the world, for any idea is simply our own projection onto life, nothing more. Psychology says this about gender: "Gender concepts are crucial to children's understanding of themselves as social beings." Gender determines a person's behavior in society and his relations with other people:

friends, colleagues, classmates, parents, casual passersby, and so on. To raise a girl as a future mother, to buy her pretty clothes and dolls and play dishes, is to project onto her and fill in for her the details of her future destiny. Through playing with dolls, a little girl practices her future role as a mother and prepares herself for what will be the main thing in her life: giving birth and caring for a child. Pretty dresses, learning to admire herself in the mirror and value her beauty will all help a girl in the future when it comes to her main natural destiny– attracting a male for fertilization. Of course, you can replace this sole, main destiny in life with any of a number of others, all of which are socially significant and important, but engaging in these others is like playing chess without striving to achieve checkmate. It's also important to raise a boy in accordance with his gender, since little boy games and similar interactions develop strength and help boys identify with the stronger sex. It isn't just physical strength that's developed, but also strength of will, which will help him conquer a girl and to protect his beloved and his hearth and home. Male and female roles aren't so clearly defined in today's world as they used to be. Even so, no one's yet been able to do away with a woman's natural purpose of bearing children and the man's natural purpose of fertilizing the female. Raising children in a gender neutral way won't cause any harm, since no matter what, assuming no one forces them to adopt certain behavioral norms, children will intuitively adopt what's right and what they need. But one thing we can be sure about is that this kind of upbringing will definitely not help a child fulfill the core destiny granted to him by his very nature.

Why Are Children Born?

You can't buy happiness. But you can give birth to it."

One time when I was in an airport, I heard the following conversation. Two passengers who happened to be on the same flight were talking, a man and a woman. The woman was flying to visit relatives in Miami for Christmas. The man asked her various questions: whether she'd lived in Canada long, whether she missed her homeland, why she was flying alone, and so on. The woman responded in a pretty animated way. It was clear that she liked her conversation partner. The man was much younger than she, and so he felt comfortable asking her very direct questions, without a trace of the caution you see in mature men. The lady told him that she always preferred to vacation alone, that only then could she fully relax. The man asked whether she was married. It turned out the woman was single. When she was asked whether she had children, she replied that she did not. The man wanted to know, why not. The woman answered that she'd made a conscious decision not to have children, that childbearing wasn't compatible with her plans, and besides, it didn't fit in with her way of life. "I love to travel, I like extreme sports, and I also have to travel a lot on business, so having children just isn't for me." When she said these words, I sensed a clear disconnect between what she was saying and what she felt inside. She was lying. She was lying not only to this total stranger, but to herself. I have no doubt that in another couple of years, this woman will give up everything – extreme sports, resort time on her own, and shopping in Miami. She'll go off in search of donor eggs – because by that time she'll no longer have any of her own left. What's more, she'll pick out the youngest woman she can find, one with good genes. She'll go about it very carefully, digging through all the donors in the data base, ferreting out the best possible candidate. By then there will be no other way to do it, because all her energy will have been spent on other endeavors.

The birth of children is a mystery. It is simply given to us without our even willing it. Of course, you can certainly plan a family, plan children, but this is planning only on the surface level. Very little depends on us. In the course of having studied various theories of child birth, and through working with many childless couples in various countries, I've come to the conclusion that whether you have a child doesn't in the least depend on whether or not you want a child. One contemporary esoteric theory states that in recent times, the number of souls wanting to incarnate is so large that they hover about, continually waiting and hoping to hurry up and latch onto any biological elements that are the least bit energetically ready to conceive. The problem with this is that there are fewer and fewer of this type of "elements," i.e. parents, all the time, because they are lacking in the necessary energy.

I'd like to focus on what approach to life drains energy and as a consequence leads to the absence of children. Giving birth requires great expenditures of energy on the part of the woman. These expenditures aren't related to the mother's physical or material circumstances, although these are present as well. Certainly, in order to bear a child, one does need physical health and material support. But what will always play the primary role is the invisible, transcendental energy that provides the reserves of physical health that are necessary to conceive and bear a child. You can call this divine energy if you like, or the energy of love (which is not to be confused with love toward the opposite sex.) Young women have a great deal of this energy, since they haven't yet expended it on trivial endeavors. It's precisely for this reason that there's a high risk of pregnancy between the ages of 15 and 25. As we age, we expend this energy on things that seem significant to us. What eats up most of it are our pleasures, particularly sexual pleasure. And having sex is not as likely to lead to infertility for men as it is for women – fertilization requires much less energy. Thus, any lady's man, ladykiller or Don Juan who takes pleasure in conquest will be able to impregnate some young thing even when he's old, and go on taking pleasure in life. But it's entirely the other way around for women. A woman's time is short. Distracting herself with sexual pleasure at all lessens the chances that she'll be able to bear a child. You can look at it figuratively this way. Think of the female childbearing energy as shagreen leather. The more sexual partners she has, the less energy she has left. The women's follicles ripen in response to her desire. If she has no desire to copulate with anyone, then she has no follicles. If she has the desire to copulate with more and more new partners, but not to give birth, then more and more follicles begin to be produced, and the supply is quickly exhausted. Questions of morality have clearly gone by the wayside in the modern world and we see, as a physical manifestation of this, that women have begun to experience early menopause. Menopause is, to be precise, the state in which the supply of follicles has been exhausted. If in the past women went through menopause roughly between the ages of 55 and 60, then now this is happening between 40 and 45. Of course, science explains this as the effect of a deteriorating ecology and female stress, while metaphysics places the blame on increasing depravity and growing desire. The desire and temptation to copulate with a new partner forces the female's ovaries to work at full speed, to produce more and more follicles. This depletes their reserve supply. Energy is wasted, and the precious follicles do their work in vain, because contraceptives are effective. Medical science has made such strides in recent years that women are now even able to check their follicular reserves any time they want, to check how many more follicles they can afford to spend on sexual pleasure and still have enough for when they do want to conceive. The AMH test allows one to determine with precision and unfailingly how much longer one can fool around. Maybe this test is indispensible for career women, but many of them don't take into account that simply having a certain quantity of follicles left is no guarantee that they'll be able to conceive. Even endless clinics offering artificial insemination won't be able to help if a woman has exhausted her spiritual energy.

If a woman sleeps with a man and is fully prepared to bear his child, then the follicular reserves aren't depleted so quickly. If a woman loves each partner – even if it's with a love that's simply the animal love of a female for a male – then she'll be able to bear children from a variety of men. But if all she wants is to get sexual pleasure from the man, to use him, then she'll become infertile very quickly, even if on the outside everything seems to be fine. Along these lines, many people often ask whether it's harmful for a woman to have sex with her husband. Sex with a regular partner isn't harmful for a woman. It's even beneficial, because she doesn't experience the same passion and attraction as when she's frequently changing partners. What's more, as paradoxical as this might seem, the families with the highest number of children are ones in which the spouses aren't sexually compatible. There's a pretty simple explanation for this: the woman isn't wasting her energy on lust, and so sex doesn't corrupt her. She doesn't feel strong attachment in this area. The film "Antichrist," by the Danish filmmaker Lars Von Trier is illuminating on this topic. A woman who has a sexual addiction (she is crazy with lust for her husband all the time) suffers the loss of her child. He dies at the very moment when she's having sex with her husband. At the end of the movie, she cruelly kills her husband. On the subconscious level, she understands that sex with him was destroying and corrupting her.

On the other hand, if a woman never experiences sexual satisfaction, then gynecological problems are unavoidable.

Children are great food fortune for any woman. To have a child means to receive a measure of love from the Almighty. Mothers with many children are awash in this love, sometimes without even realizing it. If the state of a woman's energy is not entirely in order, but not so bad, either, then the woman has the opportunity to undergo a kind of cleansing or purification before giving birth to the child. She can analyze her fate and see the course of this purification, whether this occurs before conception or the birth of the child. Before or, more often, during pregnancy, a woman experiences a whole series of misfortunes: her husband might leave her, she might suddenly fall ill, or there can be scandals in the family. As she moves through all of these difficulties, the woman passes through to a new, high level of consciousness. If she successfully makes her way along this path, then the child is more likely to be born strong and healthy. Women are often unprepared to become mothers, even though they very much want to be. But this desire alone isn't enough. She needs to have the right kind of energy: she needs to have the right relationship to the world around her, to her husband, to herself, and to her child. The older the woman is, the more disorderly and distorted her worldview will be. She'll have more complaints and will be less satisfied with her life, with herself, and with those around her. A child can't come into a world that doesn't satisfy the mother. This means that his soul will search for different, well-balanced parents. And the most well-balanced people are young people. But recently the young have been putting too many barriers to conception into place. Where can these souls who are yearning to incarnate settle?

But at the same time, it would be a mistake to see sexual promiscuity as the sole reason for childlessness. There can be a whole variety of reasons, including karmic ones. A woman might also be unable to have children because her relations with men are faulty. She might tend to use men or go to the other extreme and worship them. In the latter case, it's more likely that she'll have children. For if a woman looks down on a man, then the chance that she'll have children are practically nil. Loving the husband too strongly can also serve as an obstacle, since this is yet another stumbling block within relationships. Romantics will tell you that a child can't be born if there's no love. But there will also be no children if the woman has the wrong kind of love for her husband, if that love overshadows her love for herself and all creation. But just how measured should a woman's love for her husband be so that it won't overshadow and close off the flow of the energy she needs to bear a child? That's a separate topic. Overall, the topic of childlessness is a huge and fascinating topic for research, but in this chapter I'm only touching on the most important and common reasons women are unable to bear children.

    In the course of my work, I encountered one couple that had been trying desperately to get pregnant for five years. But all their attempts and inducements ended in failure. Despairing, they turned to a clinic that offered artificial insemination. They were told that their case was hopeless, since the woman had difficulties with her fallopian tubes, and the only option was to implant an embryo. But the pair was destined to be disappointed yet again. The implanted embryo didn't survive. The body rejected it, and the pregnancy ended in miscarriage. The doctors suggested they try again. But the family refused. But then, two years later, the woman became pregnant naturally. What had happened? A miracle called acceptance. The couple had learned the lesson they'd needed to learn: they'd made peace with the fact that they'd never have children and began living in the present rather than the future. The pregnancy happened when they were no longer actively wanting and expecting it. When the point of the trail has been grasped and no longer needs to be learned, then the trial has been successfully passed and the need for further testing vanishes.

It often happens that a couple is unable to get pregnant because they're too timid in their relationship with each other: they're striving to maintain propriety and a good tone in their interactions, and what lies behind these efforts is their desire to always appear good to each other and to themselves. There's no sincerity in this kind of relationship. Both parties are like martyrs who have been bound together for eternity by fate. All it will take for the wife to immediately have a child is to leave and find a different partner, one who's less delicate, who's even crude at times. But the difficulty is that before she can leave, she has to clearly see the situation as it is. And in order to do this, she has to be herself, free of games, and she has to stop seeking comfort in life. But the sad thing is, that it's practically impossible for her to remember who she is beneath this years long game.

You'll find a great variety of life situations. There's no need to try to make someone else's situation fit you. But the one important and undeniable point is that we're given children not because we behave well or think correctly, and not because we love someone. They're given to us when we're ready for them inside, when we're prepared to feel compassion, to live through life with them, to sacrifice for them. When a woman isn't ready for this inside, then none of her attempts at pregnancy will be successful, even if she tries artificial insemination. No matter how hard the doctors try, the pregnancy will end. The same thing happens with childless couples who want to adopt a child. If the family is not ready for a child, the adoption won't be successful. A whole series of obstacles is sure to arise on the path. My own experience in the course of many years of working with adoptive parents has shown me this: if a family comes to an orphanage to adopt a child and they already have their own biological children, then the adoption usually moves forward smoothly and quickly, without a hitch. If I read a couple's dossier and see that they're childless, that they've undergone years of infertility treatment and have attempted artificial insemination with no success and decided on adoption out of despair, then it's already clear to me that my work with them will not be easy. There have been cases in which the judge had already issued a decree to allow the adoption and only one day remained until the child's departure, and then the biological mother turned up, and the would be adoptive parents left empty-handed. As long as the woman's suffering over her infertility hasn't been exhausted or worked through, as long as she doesn't accept it and hasn't submitted to it, then it's unlikely that anything will fall into place. But sometimes the opposite happens: when the couple makes peace with the fact that they'll never have their own children and comes to adopt a child, then they can end up having biological children in short order, too, even without medical intervention. In my practice I had dealings with a wonderful couple from Belgium. For many years the family had been childless, and the doctors said everything was hopeless. They adopted a little girl. Then, a year later, they sent me a photo of twins. My first thought was that they'd conceived artificially. And I thought, why did they do that? If they really wanted a second child, they could have made it possible for yet another orphan to have a family. I wrote to them. It turned out that they hadn't even suspected that the wife was pregnant. It came as a great surprise even to them. Now this happy family is raising three girls, in defiance of all the medical diagnoses.

Appendix with Games

Children's games occupy a special place in a child's life. And they ought to play just as important spot in the lives of adults. We need to play with our children constantly. And to do that we need to think up games that will be interesting for the adults, too. Then they'll become irreplaceable family favorites. Nothing brings a family together like playing games with each other. Children adore playing with adults, and if the chance to do this comes up, they'll choose it even over time with their friends. That doesn't mean that playing with adults should entirely crowd out a child's interactions with his peers, but even so, they should become an alternate way for the child to pass his time.

The games I include below are ones we thought up in our family to play in our free time. I can't claim that they're educational or that they'll develop the children or are particularly useful. We play them just because they're fun to play. We play for the fun of it, without having any goals in mind. Both the children and we, the parents, like them. They shorten the long winter evenings. All the same, there is one benefit of the games: when the kids' friends call and invite them to go somewhere, they pause and ask us, "What are we going to play today?" In other words, they're deciding whether to go somewhere with their friends or stay home. That's an indication that it's just as interesting for the children to be at home as it is for them to be with their friends.

Our family has two favorite board games. One is Russian Lotto. It's something like bingo, but differs in that the leader has little wooden barrels that he holds in his hand. The leader calls out the number on the barrel and the players watch their cards. We love to play lotto when we have guests. Our neighbors often drop in specifically to play this game, since in Canada they've never seen anything like

Russian Lotto. This game is interesting to play with a lot of people, and it's also more fun to beat others in the game instead of just members of the family.

Our second favorite board game is "1,000." The whole family loves to play it. It's a complicated game, requiring both sharp attention and mathematical quickness. Sometimes we get into arguments and have to sort things out, but we love it all the same. We play for a small amount of money. It's a common game, so I won't detail the rules here.

But I will describe our other games, the one's we've thought up for our family relaxation. Probably every family has a game or two that defies explanation. These may be not so much games, as mischief that verges on hooliganism. Parents should definitely be mischievous with their children. When our family began discussing what games I should include in this book, the children suggested including the naughtiest ones because they're such big fans of them. Of course I didn't include them. But we're happy to share our other games.

Concert

I'll start off by saying that no one in our family has any talents whatsoever. We're the most ordinary and average individuals. No one has any musical talent, no one writes poetry or takes part in any performances. Nonetheless, at home, within our family circle, we allow ourselves to really cut loose, in spite of the fact that when we first organized these family concerts, no one particularly wanted to take part in all of this. No one felt like thinking up anything, much less show what they'd come up with. When I first issued the challenge for each of us to prepare our own musical number and then perform it for all the other family members – who would then score each number – no one showed much enthusiasm for the idea. Really, they greeted the whole idea with hostility. "Why a concert?" the boys howled. "Don't we have anything better to do?" Even their desire to win some tasty prizes couldn't win them over. It's difficult explain what motivates them now, their continuing desire for tasty snacks, or an interest in creative pursuits. But in any case, it's now the children who announce each concert date and beg me not to put it off. You see, I'm always rescheduling it, because I'm always chronically short on time to prepare my number. Even so, we still manage to put on these concerts regularly, once a month. All you need to play "concert" is at least three people. You can have more, but no fewer. Give each person five pieces of paper of identical size, on which you've written the numerals one through five on separate sheets. So, if three people are playing, you'll have three sheets with the number 1, the same number of sheets with the number 2, and so on. You'll need the sheets for scoring the performances according to a five-point scale. The jury members each comment on their score, share their opinions about the number and their suggestions for improvement. It's no problem if only three people are playing. It doesn't make the concert any less interesting.

    If you want, you can choose an emcee, whose job is to introduce the performer in a beautiful and intriguing way. Each person prepares his number on his own, in secret. My job is to prepare prizes. If three people are playing, then there are three prizes, and if there are more participants, then you should prepare a prize for each person. But each prize should differ in terms of cost. We usually buy yummy chocolates. The first place winner wins the biggest chocolate, or two chocolates (there's no limit to what you can think up here.) The prize for second place is a more modest chocolate, the third place prize is a bit smaller than that, and so on. If there are four players, then award an Encouragement Prize; if there are five, then add in a Grand Prize. No one should go without a prize, which encourages each player to prepare for the next concert more carefully and creatively. The one who accumulates the highest number of points wins the first prize. We advise each participant to prepare two numbers, because it often happens that the voting ends in a tie. If this happens, the players have the chance to perform a second number. The kids are often tricky and don't show the score they're awarding until the person next to them shows his, so that they have time to do a count and see who's scored how many points, so as to ensure their own victory. Because after all, the participants are also the members of the jury! This is the whole beauty of the game. It's a test of honesty and objectivity. The best approach is to establish a strict order of announcing the scores, and to stick to it. If someone scores someone else way too low– and usually the kids do this to me, especially when my number ends up being the best – then we put a stop to the concerts and don't reinstate them until an honest score is posted. In order to encourage objectivity, you can also use secret voting. Since we are constantly introducing new rules and improving the game, we've managed to ensure that the concerts are lots of fun and honest, and no one gets offended. The numbers can consist of any type of performance, even shooting at a target with a bow and arrow. All in all, to each his own. I advise parents to put on these concerts at home on the most ordinary days, for no reason at all. It really brings everyone together and provides a lot of enjoyment, for parents and children alike.

Learning to Speak Eloquently

This game came about in our family more out of necessity than as a fun way to spend our time. At one time our sons got into the habit of using English slang. They would pepper each other with phrases that had no real meaning whatsoever. Some of these words just began to suck the life out of the language. As often happens, when they began studying English, the boys really took a liking to the slang in particular, rather than the literary language. It seemed cool to them to use phrases like "Dude," "What the hell?", "Shit!" and so on. They delighted in using them. What's more, whenever they would get into an argument, each of them had words in their arsenal that were particularly hurtful to the other. And they both knew how to use them when they were arguing. I took it upon myself to teach the children to express themselves eloquently during any disagreements. In order to achieve this, at the beginning of each week, I'd do a presentation, in the course of which I would acquaint them with the rules of behavior for the week. On the bulletin board in the hall, I'd hang up a poster, divided into two sides. One half belonged to my older son, and on that half I'd note down a set of words that my younger son particularly disliked. For example, my younger son detested the words and phrases "little," "don't cry, little boy," "Mama's boy," and so on. On the second side of the poster, the side belonging to my younger son, I noted down words and phrases my older son didn't like. I'd set aside ten dollars for each son throughout the course of the event, which would usually last for ten days. I'd make one check on the poster each time I heard them utter one of the forbidden words or phrases. Each mark indicated the loss of one dollar. At the event's end, we'd count up the marks on each son's side and subtract them from the ten dollars. In this way, each of them would earn some money by practicing self-control and being attentive. I have to say that at first, they were sneaky. For example, instead of saying, "little," they'd say, "awful," and argue that this word wasn't on the list, and that what wasn't on the forbidden list was permitted. Or, say, they'd replace "idiot" with "idiod" and would try to prove that it was an entirely different word, which meant they could keep the dollar. Each week we'd update and improve the word list. Then we added an additional list of expressions whose use we would, on the contrary, *encourage* financially. For example, "Let's find a way to compromise," or "I'm prepared to hear you out. Let's hear your decision," or "What's our consensus?" (which was particularly appropriate during fights over things.) The results astounded me. The children began to like these cryptic words and began using them. At first they would laugh when they uttered them, then bravado replaced the laughter. Within about three months, we had no more need of these presentations. The children began speaking to each other totally normally, and if a slang word slipped in now and again, out of habit, then no one would react at all. And when no one reacts to a word, then the speaker stops using it. In this way we learned to respect each other's ears and to value pure and beautiful speech.

Border Crossing

This game is for children aged 4-8. We don't play this one with our whole family, and it hasn't become such a part of our family culture. We play it only with our younger son. Everyone else just watches and occasionally shouts out a guess. In this game, one person demonstrates some animal's habits, all without words, and the other person guesses what animal it is. We usually play this on weekend mornings, lying in bed. This game will probably not work for parents who don't allow their children to climb into bed with them. If that's the case, you can modify the game. The game setup is that you're at the border. The border guard – the person guessing the animal – stands on the border, i.e., he lies in the bed. On one side of him is a thick forest, on the other a city. The border guard's task is to not let the animals, who are constantly striving to make their way into the city, get past the border, in other words, past him. The guard has to guess the animal's identity in time; he has to decide quickly whether to let the given animal through or not and decide whether or not it might harm the peaceful inhabitants of the city. The game requires a knowledge of the animal world, of animals' habits and of course, a quick reaction time. The guard has to be able to judge by appearance alone what kind of animal stands before him, identify it and, if it poses a threat to the peaceful city-dwellers, put it to sleep by shooting it with an imaginary pistol. If the animal wishing to cross the border is a bunny that wanted to have a tasty dinner in someone's garden, or a squirrel, you can't put them to sleep, but you can't let a bear or a wolf into the city. Children generally don't like to play the role of the border guard, preferring to imitate the beasts and clamber over the adults to the other side of the border. It's more fun for them that way. Adults, on the other hand, prefer to be border guards. After all, you can loll about in bed longer and play with your child at the same time. But of course, it's better to switch the roles now and then.

Mice

We've been playing this game for three years now. The game has turned out to have no end, and if we managed to write down the whole scenario and animated it, then we might end up with a very funny cartoon about the adventures of two brave mice. I'll just give you a general outline of the game so that parents will have an idea of how you can play role-playing games of this type. You'll definitely make the game your own, with your own heroes and your own scenario. The scenario develops on its own, as you go along. You don't need to think anything up beforehand, or else it will be boring. Each player, grownups and children alike, uses two fingers to simulate a person walking down the road. Give the little person a name, and he becomes your constant friend in any situation. In our game, these are not little people at all, but two jolly baby mice who are always with us. No matter where my son and I might be, if we're bored and our hands are free, we start playing "mice." We think up the scenarios as we go along, a new one each time, not connected to any previous story. Our little mice have already been in outer space, they've visited Santa Claus, they've outsmarted a dumb bear, and have done many brave deeds. It just so happens that one of our mice is more careful and cowardly. It's not hard to guess whose it was – mine, naturally. But my son's baby mouse is the opposite, the picture of bravery, cunning and courage. Games like these develop a child's imagination and help pass the time when you're waiting.

Automatic Writing

Automatic writing is a method of working with the subconscious to receive whatever information you wish.

Automatic writing is a parapsychology term that refers to the individual's ability to compose comprehensible writings without consciously controlling the process. At the same time as he's doing the automatic writing, the person can be engaged in some totally separate activity and not even realize what he's writing. Based on scientific investigation, researchers have concluded that we can think of automatic writing as access to the unconscious that we gain in certain circumstances. In our family, we don't use automatic writing to get any information or for its therapeutic effect. We don't try to do actual automatic writing. We're just playing and imitating it. The whole family plays. And in fact, our younger son began playing this game with us even before he even learned to write, although you do need to be able to write in order to play. He learned to play it orally and would make everything up in his head. And he ended up doing no worse than those of us who were using pen and paper. True, he'd sometimes forget what he'd wanted to say, but even then, he wouldn't be thrown off – he'd just think up something new on the fly, and it would turn out even funnier.

Here's how to play: in each round of play, one person says a word, any word he wants. As soon as the word is pronounced, the players pick up their pens and, after writing down the first word that comes into their heads. The point of the game is to write down everything that comes to mind without thinking at all about what you're writing. The point is to not think. If suddenly your pen stops, then your writing is done, and you shout, "Stop!" The remaining players have to put down their pens. Everyone reads aloud what they've written. You'll get very funny and absurd results. You'll often end up with rhymed couplets or quatrains, or, in some cases, prose. The pen gives birth to amazing things.

Towns

This game is for older children. If a child is playing with the adults, then you need to use a different scoring system for him. For example, if everyone else earns 10 points for each right answer, then give the child 20 points, so that there's no big discrepancy in point totals. This is a cerebral game. Each player takes a sheet of paper and draws several columns on it, which they then label "towns," "plants," "animals," "makes of cars," and "points." Put a newspaper in the middle of the table. Go around clockwise. The players take turns closing their eyes and pointing to any letter in the newspaper. As soon as each letter is chosen, each player must write down a city, plant, animal and make of car that begins with that letter. Whoever finishes first shouts, "Stop!" and all the other players put down their pens. Then you check the answers. Everyone totals up how many answers they managed to write down, and gives themselves 10 points for each answer. If players have both written the same word, then they each receive 5 points. Then you add up the total points earned for each letter and note that down in the "points" column. At the end of the game we count up the grand total of points each person has earned, and based on the results we announce who is the "Scholar of the Evening." If you'd like, you can have some small prizes on hand. But we're usually perfectly happy to play without any prizes at all. The children like the actual process of picking the letters, the writing, and totaling up the points.

Puffy

This is a very noisy game, and when my younger son and I are playing and we really get into our roles, then everyone else shuts their doors. We named it "puffy" for the simple reason that this was the first thing that came into our heads. You'll think up your own character and use whatever name you like. Our "Puffy" is a large, kind, imaginary creature. The only thing we know about her is that she speaks in a very loud voice. In our family I play the role of "Puffy." When I play that role, I distort my voice in a fun way and speak very loudly. As loudly as I possibly can. Puffy always shows up unexpectedly; we never decide to play "Puffy." She just shows up when the mood strikes, or when I need to cheer my son up. Puffy is very noisy and jolly. She asks lots of questions and runs away at top speed. We don't play "Puffy" for more than 5 or 6 minutes, but that's more than enough to liven up the evening or to share some important and serious information with my child. When Puffy shows up, my son immediately starts asking her questions: where do you live, why do you speak so loudly, what are you like, why do you disappear so quickly? This really amuses us both.

Concentration

I'm not a big fan of games psychologists have developed specifically to develop one's powers of concentration or observation or memory. These games aren't popular in our family, despite the fact that several of them are certainly worthy of our attention. I don't doubt that they're useful, but you won't ever end up playing them more than once, because the kids get bored.

One good game for the powers of observation is to give a child a sheet of paper and colored pencils and to ask him to draw ten triangles in a row. When he's done that, warn the child that he should pay careful attention to the instructions you'll now give, since you'll repeat them only once. Here are the instructions: "Carefully color in the third, seventh and ninth triangles with red." If the child asks for clarification, tell him that he should do whatever he understood you to say. If the child succeeds in carrying out the first set of instructions, you can continue with steadily more complicated tasks.

An exercise to develop the powers of observation

Offer this game to your child. Tell him, "Look around the room careful and find the objects that have a circle in them or are circular. The child names the items – watches, a doorknob, a table, etc. You can make a competition out of it, to see who can name the most objects.

A game to develop the memory

The object of this game is to continue a thought and to recall who has said what. An adult begins the game and says, "I put some apples in the sack." The child repeats what's been said and then adds something he's thought up:

"I put apples and bananas in the sack." Whoever has the next turn repeats the whole phrase and adds something. You can simply add one word each, or you can also choose words in alphabetical order.

No yes or no, no black or white, no bow-shaped mouth

This game is very widespread, and probably everyone has played it at one time or another. It develops one's concentration. But it's best not to get too carried away with this game, or else your child might get into the habit of always thinking before he says something. Many people think that's a good and correct habit. But if you're trying to develop a child's feelings, his ability to show them and not be shy about expressing himself, then you need to stress sincerity, spontaneity and openness. The brain will soak all of up in two seconds. This is a game to develop the mind, to train it, which is why you shouldn't get so carried away with it.

To play, start talking with the child on any topic that interests him. His job is to answer but to make sure that he doesn't use the words yes, no, black, or white. And you aren't allowed to "make your mouth into a bow," i.e., to laugh. It's also good to switch roles and give your child the chance to ask you questions.

Glue fantasies

Collect in a box anything that can be glued onto paper. This can be pieces of cotton, fabric, napkins, things you've cut out of old newspapers and magazines, twigs, tree leaves, plastic bag ties, tiny beads, in short, anything you want. The child will have a great time gluing all of this onto paper. But you'll need to help him figure out what will be the centerpiece, which objects will be central. If you've cut out pictures of animate beings or animals from magazines, then they'll be the main characters, and everything else will go around them. If he's using inanimate objects, then there's no end to the forms the fantasy can take.

Playing with books

All children love to look at the pictures in books. You can play this game with your child. Look at a given picture in a book and then turn the page. Ask your child to tell you what he remembers about what the picture showed. You can help him by asking questions. You can think up all manner of questions based on the picture.

Stuffed toys

All children love stuffed toys. Of course, they play with them only very rarely. As a rule, a child will quickly get tired of a stuffed animal and forget about it. It's better not to buy large stuffed animals, since although they're pretty, it's not easy to play with them. That kind of toy will function more as an accessory to the child's room than an object for play. Children's tastes tend more toward small brightly colored toys that they can easily hold in their hands. Children are usually very happy to play with them. When a stuffed toy does show up in the home, you should animate it, name it, and talk with it now and then. Then the child will be more interested in playing with that toy. We really like small puppets that fit easily on your hand. Don't buy too many, or the child will lose interest in them. It's better to buy two or three and play with them periodically. Our two finger puppets have practically become members of the family. There's Quack the duckling and Moo the cow, who are always inseparable. And we ourselves are inseparable from them. Even when we go on vacation, they're the first to end up in the suitcase. There's a great variety of ways you can play with stuffed toys. You can even use them in games that develop the memory or concentration. For example, you can put several stuffed toys in a row. Have the child remember their positions and then close his eyes for several minutes. While his eyes are closed you can change their positions. You can have them switch places, or raise one's paws, or tip one's head to the side. Then ask the child to tell you what's changed with the animals.

Tests

I've included in the book several entertaining tests developed by leading 20th century psychologists. These tests can help parents understand their child better. Some of the tests are for parents. They'll help parents determine how correct their approach to child rearing is. Unfortunately, I haven't been able to determine who developed every test. They've been reworked and expanded by various psychologists over the course of many years, and in some cases it's impossible to identify a test's original authors.

What's your child's character type?

This test was developed by the Volkovs, Russian psychologists. Its essence is as follows: you answer the following questions and draw your own conclusions.

1. **How does your child behave in situations where quick action is required?**
   a) He easily shifts into action
   b) He takes action energetically
   c) He acts calmly, with few words
   d) He acts timidly, with uncertainty

2. **How does your child react to a teacher's corrections?**
   a) He says that he won't do whatever it is again, but before long does the same thing again
   b) He pays no attention and does what he wants; he reacts to the correction in a heated manner
   c) He hears the teacher out in silence
   d) He says nothing, feels hurt, and is upset

3. **How does your child interact with other children in situations that are important to him?**
   a) Quickly, excitedly, but he also listens to what others have to say
   b) Quickly and passionately, without listening to others
   c) Slowly and calmly, but confidently
   d) With great uncertainty

4. **How does he behave in unfamiliar circumstances (in the doctor's office, with administrators, etc.)?**
   a) He gets his bearings easily and is engaged
   b) He takes an active part and shows heightened excitement
   c) He's calm and takes in his surroundings
   d) He's timid and is thrown off

Key:
If you answered mostly "a", then you're dealing with a sanguine personality;
Mostly "b" indicates a choleric personality;
Mostly "c" indicates a phlegmatic personality;
Mostly "d" indicates a melancholy temperament.

What kind of relationship do you have with your child?

Choose the answers that fit best.

1. **If your child flunked a test in school, what will you do?**
   a) I'll give him a good dressing down and make him sit home and cram 2
   b) I'll help him figure out the new subject matter and learn the material 3
   c) If he didn't pass this one, he'll pass the next one. It's no big deal 1
   d) I'll go to the school and give the teacher a piece of my mind 4

2. **If your child takes some money without asking and spends it all, what will you do?**
   a) I'll punish him 2
   b) I'll have a discussion with him and try to explain where he's gone wrong 3
   c) Let him take it; I'm working for his sake 4
   d) Money doesn't grow on trees 1

3. **How much time do you spend with your child each day?**
   a) The bare minimum 2
   b) A great deal 4
   c) All my free time! 3
   d) I have no spare time to spend with him 1

4. **Did you read your child bedtime stories?**
   a) Regularly 3
   b) Rarely 1
   c) Never, but my spouse would read to him 0
   d) Why stuff a child's head with that kind of thing before bed? 2

5. **How does your family spend summer vacations?**

a) Dad goes west, Mom goes south, and the kids go to camp! 1
   b) We try to always be together: at home, on hikes and at the beach 3
   c) We send the kids to the relatives or camp 2
   d) The child can go wherever he wants 4

6. **How often do you give your children advice?**
   a) Every minute 2
   b) Children know what to do without my help 4
   c) When the need arises 3
   d) I don't think anyone should ever give anyone advice 1

7. **After an argument who makes up first?**
   a) The person who's first to realize he was wrong 3
   b) No one ever does 1
   c) Of course it should be the child, because he's younger 2
   d) It's always me – I feel sorry for him! 4

8. **Does your child trust you with his secrets?**
   a) In his most open moments, yes 3
   b) I find out everything from the neighbors and friends 4
   c) Why do I need to know his secrets? That's why they're secrets - because you don't share them 1
   d) He can't *not* tell me. If I press him, he'll tell me everything 2

9. **Do you try to fulfill all your child's wishes?**
   a) Of course, every single one 4
   b) Yes, if I have the time and the resources 3
   c) Wishes – yes, capricious desires – no 2

    d) Children should fulfill their parents' wishes 1

10. **Are you capable of handing your child over to an official institution or relatives for an extended period (more than a month)?**
    a) Only if circumstances require it 3
    b) That's precisely what I do 2
    c) No way 4
    d) Let him do what he wants 1

Note down your answers and tally up your points.

Total points 10-15: You consider children a by-product of your life that came from who knows where. Your point of departure in your relationship with your children is the motto "I want to live for myself!" You live your life, and there's no place in it for your child. Your cool treatment of your child means that he doesn't develop a strong attachment to you. With each passing year, you grow further and further apart. Your everyday interactions bring no warmth or joy. All that connects you are material matters. Once your child gains independence you may experience total estrangement. Neither of you will want to see each other.

Total points 16-25: You are totally convinced that you're the head of the family. Therefore the child should definitely listen to you and carry out all your demands without the slightest hesitation. Your pronouncements are the last word on everything. You have little interest in the child's opinions, interests, or problems. You have a clear plan for how to raise and educate your child. Any resistance on the part of the child to your furious decrees only makes matters worse. Since he's incapable of standing up to you, the child tries to distance himself from the constant conflict, goes inside himself and silently hears out his parent's furious moralizing. It's possible that in the future, once he manages to get out from under your tenacious surveillance, this "obedient" child will end up doing exactly the opposite of what you've taught him to do all those years. Just to spite you.

Total points 26-34: You have a trusting relationship with your child. You're in the loop about all of his little joys and disappointments. Your child considers you a close friend and tries not to upset you in his words or actions. But if he does upset you, then you'll make up quickly, and the conflict won't turn into a protracted internecine war. You're confident in your child's actions and can predict how he'll behave in this or that situation. The child sees in you a reliable support and defense. You speak to each other as equals and don't resort to primitive personal attacks. You hold your child to standards and are appropriately strict with your child. Your relationship is built on mutual respect.

Total points 35-40: Your child openly orders you around. By fulfilling his every capricious desire from the time he was little, you've willingly become his servant. As he grows up, he'll be less and less likely to take your opinion into account. You risk raising an egotist. The child is fully convinced that the whole universe revolves around him. At some point in the future, Copernicus will come along and explain how the world really is organized and turn your child's worldview on its head. But will that even help? How can you be sure…

What's your family's biofield?

Answer "yes" or "no":

1. Our family is very friendly.
2. On Saturdays and Sundays we tend to eat breakfast, lunch and dinner all together.

3. The presence of several of my family members usually throws me out of balance.
4. I feel very comfortable in my own home.
5. There are some circumstances in our family life that are very destabilizing for our relationships.
6. I relax best at home.
7. If disagreements occur in our family, then they're quickly forgotten.
8. Some of my family members' habits really annoy me.
9. I have every basis for considering my home my castle.
10. When guests come to visit, it usually has a very positive effect on family relations.
11. There is a very unstable person in our family.
12. There is at least one person in my family who always comforts or inspires me or cheers me up.
13. There are one or more family members who are very difficult people.
14. Everyone in our family understands each other well.
15. We've noticed that when guests come, the visits are usually accompanied by small or significant conflicts within the family.
16. When I'm away from home for long, I really miss my "home sweet home."
17. When friends visit us they usually remark on how calm and peaceful things are in our family.
18. From time to time our family experiences great trouble.
19. The atmosphere at home often has a depressing effect on me.
20. I consider myself alone in the family and not needed by anyone.
21. We usually vacation all together in the summer.
22. We usually do the household chores as a group – cleaning the house, holiday preparations, work at the summer house, etc.

23. Our family members often sing or play musical instruments.
24. A joyful and jolly atmosphere reigns in our house.
25. The situation at home is more often painful, sad or tense.
26. It's annoying to me that everyone or nearly everyone in the house speaks with raised voices.
27. It's customary in our family for family members to apologize to each other when they've made a mistake or caused each other discomfort.
28. We usually have a jolly get-together on holidays.
29. Things are so uncomfortable in my family that I often don't feel like going home.
30. People often insult me at home.
31. I'm always pleased that things are in good order in our apartment.
32. When I come home I often find that I don't feel like seeing or hearing anyone.
33. Relations in our family are extremely tense.
34. I know that someone in our family feels uncomfortable.
35. We often have guests come to visit.

Now let's count the number of correct answers. Give yourself one point for each correct answer. You should have answered "Yes" to questions 1, 2, 4, 6, 7, 9, 10, 12, 14, 16, 17, 21, 22, 23, 24, 27, 28, 31 and 35, and "No" to questions 3, 5, 8, 11, 13, 15, 18, 19, 20, 25, 29, 30, 32, 33 and 34.

If you scored from 0-8 points, then that's an alarming indicator. Your family has a negative biofield. Families in this range include those that have decided on divorce or those that consider their life together "difficult," "unbearable," or "a nightmare." A score of 9-15 is characteristic of spouses who are occasionally disappointed in their life together and who experience a certain amount of tension. A score of 16-22 points is characteristic of families in which you can see certain unhealthy factors, but in which positive energy predominates.

If you scored between 23 and 35 points, it means your family has a good biofield.

How good are your parenting skills?

Unfortunately, there's disagreement about who came up with this test, even though it's entirely unique. Some sources claim a French psychologist developed it, while others say it was an English psychologist. But what makes the test unique is that it's also informative and contains information that will help parents make better child-raising decisions.

Answer "yes" or "no" to each question.

1. Girls are more obedient than boys.

2. Girls like nature more than boys do.

3. Boys are better at sizing up a complex situation and think more logically.

4. Boys feel more of a desire to excel.

5. Boys are more gifted at math.

6. Girls are more sensitive to the atmosphere they live in and have a harder time bearing pain and suffering.

7. Girls are better at expressing their thoughts.

8. Boys have a better visual memory, while girls have a better aural memory.

9. Boys have a better sense of direction.

10. Boys are more aggressive.

11. Girls are less active.

12. Girls are more sociable, prefer large groups to a small circle of friends.

13. Girls are more affectionate.

14. Girls fall under others' influence more easily.

15. Boys are more innovative.

16. Girls are more cowardly.

17. Girls more often suffer from low self-esteem.

Correct answers

1. In early childhood girls really are more obedient.

2. Although nothing along these lines has yet been proven, the following may give reason to conclude that this is the case: by nature girls are more likely to take care of sick and weak animals and plants, but only between the ages of 6 and 9.

3. This is not the case. Girls can complete complex tasks (problems) no worse than boys.

4. Before age 10-12 girls develop more quickly (and for this reason sometimes strive to stand out and distinguish themselves from their peers.) But after this, girls are more goal-oriented and think more about the future than boys.

5. Girls and boys are equally gifted. Everything depends on how we focus them, although it's thought that boys perform better in math. But when we take this preconception out of the picture, then we don't see a big difference.

6. On the contrary, boys are more drawn into their surroundings and therefore feel separation from their parents more keenly. Boys are more sensitive to pain and suffering. It's just that on the outside they pretend that they're not in pain, since from the time they're little they're taught that men shouldn't cry.

7. Until ages 10-13, the difference is insignificant, after which time in the majority of cases girls express themselves more precisely than boys, both orally and in writing.

8. Research has shown that over the course of their entire lives, girls' and boys' capacities are the same. Any difference is purely individual.

9. Before the onset of puberty, there is no difference, but after that, boys have a better sense of direction. The difference grows over time. Exceptions only prove the rule.

10. Boys become aggressive at a very early age, at age 2 or 3, when their personality begins to form.

11. No difference in activity levels of boys and girls has been established. It's just that in childhood, boys are noisier and obviously active (as when they're fighting, for example.) At the same time, while girls are not as noisy, they are no less goal-oriented.

12. On the contrary, girls prefer to have one close friend, or perhaps no more than two, rather than a large group. This is why it's boys who get together in larger groups. This situation continues into adulthood, and it's for this reason that boys are more inclined to play group games.

13. Until they reach a certain age there's no difference between boys and girls in this area, and at a certain point boys seek affection.

14. On the contrary, boys tend more toward accepting group opinion "on faith," which we definitely need to take into account in raising them. Girls generally stick to their own opinions.

15. As far as this quality is concerned, there's no difference between boys and girls up to a certain age. Later on girls become more aware and active. But during the period of sexual maturation, girls allow boys to dominate in this area. Perhaps consciously.

16. Girls are actually not as cowardly as many people think. In actual fact they can be stronger and more decisive than boys and have an easier time conquering fear.

17. Not any more so than boys. Girls are better «armed» to cope with complex life situations and know how to adapt more quickly.

Are you a leader or a follower?

The following questions can help you determine what your nature is: someone who guides or is guided, a leader or a follower? Answer "Yes," "No," or "I don't know" to each question.

1. I always feel responsible for all that happens in my life.
2. I wouldn't have so many problems if certain people changed how they treated me.
3. I prefer to take action rather than to reflect on the reasons for my failures.
4. It sometimes seems to me that I was born "under an unlucky star."
5. Alcoholics' disease is their own fault.
6. I sometimes think that the people who have influenced who I am and the way I grew up are responsible for much in my life.
7. If I come down with a cold, I prefer to treat myself on my own.
8. Other people are most often to blame if a woman has the annoying qualities of being aggressive or quarrelsome.
9. There's a solution to any problem.
10. I enjoy helping others because I feel grateful for what others have done for me.
11. If a conflict arises, then when I'm reflecting on whose fault it is, I generally start with myself.
12. If a black cat crosses my path, I cross to the other side of the street.

13. Everyone should be strong and independent, no matter what the circumstances.
14. I know my weaknesses, but I want others to be tolerant of them.
15. I usually make my peace with situations I have no power to control.

For each "yes" answer to questions 1, 3, 5, 6, 9, 11 and 13, and for each "no" answer to questions 2, 4, 6, 8, 10, 12, 14 and 15, give yourself 10 points. For each "I don't know", give yourself 5 points.

100-150 points: You are the "captain" of your own life. You feel responsible for all that happens to you, you take a great deal on yourself, overcome difficulties without exaggerating them or elevating them to the status of major life's problems.

50-99 points: You're happy to "steer", but if necessary, you're capable of passing the wheel to reliable hands. Flexibility, reason and tact are your constant companions.

Less than 49 points: You easily submit to external forces. You'll blame anyone but yourself for your difficulties. True independence seems unattainable to you.

How cautious are you?

Some people are overly cautious and think things over excessively. Before doing anything, they'll "measure 7 times." Others prefer risk. They're able to bet the bank. They're always putting on the gas, they make quick decisions and rarely regret them. This test will help you determine which category you fall into.

1. Are you afraid of making people angry if you know they're physically stronger than you?
2. Do you cause a scene to get others to pay attention to you?
3. Do you like to drive fast even if it puts your life at risk?
4. Do you like taking medicine when you get sick?
5. Are you capable of doing anything in order to get what you want?
6. Do you like large dogs?
7. Do you like to sit in the sun for hours at a time?
8. Are you convinced that someday you'll become famous?
9. Are you able to stop yourself in time if you feel that you're beginning to lose?
10. Are you accustomed to eating a lot, even if you're not hungry?
11. Do you like to know beforehand what gifts people will give you?

Now let's tally your score.

Give yourself one point for each "yes" answer you gave for questions 2 and 10 and one point for each negative answer you gave to questions 1, 3, 4, 5, 6, 8, 9, and 11.

More than 9 points: You are wisdom incarnate. You are rational and your needs are modest. Although it wouldn't hurt you to put on a little more gas. That will lighten your interactions with others and make life a little simpler.

4-8 points: The golden middle. You have a marvelous sense of measure. You know exactly what you're capable of and don't go chasing windmills. Although you do tend to be a bit extravagant, which lends people a bit of charm!

Less than 4 points: There's only one thing to say: you are absolutely reckless. Nothing is ever enough for you. For this reason you are not satisfied with your life. You're always rushing off somewhere. Learn to take joy in the little niceties of life, of which there are quite a few. That will help you become calmer and more sensible.

Psycho Geometric test

People first started talking about psycho geometry in the United States. The author of this test is Susan Dellinger. Her test is a most unique system for personality analysis. The conclusions you can reach by using psycho geometry are 85% reliable. This is an abridged presentation of the description of the shapes, but the main traits are preserved.

It's very easy to do this test with children. Children generally name their figure very quickly, while adults often get thrown off and start to think and change their answers, so that in the final analysis, they aren't able to clearly associate themselves with any one figure. Look at the following figures:

Pick the one about which you can say, "That's me!" Try to feel your form. If you have a great deal of trouble doing this, pick the figure that first attracted your attention.

Write down the name of this figure and label it number 1. Now pick the remaining figured and arrange them in order of your preference, labeling them with the corresponding numbers.

The most difficult part is done.

The figure you put in first place is your basic figure. It will enable you to determine your main, dominating character traits and behavioral fine points.

The remaining four figures are the distinctive companions that can color your behavior.

The last figure indicates the shape of the kind of person with whom you'll find it most difficult to interact.

However, it can turn out that no one figure fits you entirely. In that case, a combination of two or even three figures might provide the best description of you.

Square

If your main figure is the square, then you are a tireless toiler. A strong work ethic, effort and the need to finish what you start, a stubbornness that enable you to complete your work are the main qualities of true Squares. Endurance, patience and a methodical approach usually make Squares first class specialists in their areas of expertise. This is also aided by their unceasing need for information. More often than not, everything in their heads is carefully filed. A Square can give you any necessary information at a moment's notice. For this reason Squares have the reputation of being erudite, at least in their area of specialty.

Squares are more likely to "compute a result" than guess what it will be. They are exceedingly attentive to details and fine points and love to bring everything into final and perfect order. Their ideal life is a well-planned out and predictable life, and they do not like changes in the usual order of events. They are constantly "putting things in order" and organizing the people and things around them.

All these qualities make it possible for Squares to become good experts – technicians and excellent administrators, but they are rarely good managers. Their excessive fondness for detail and their need to have clarifying information deprives Squares of efficiency. In Squares attention to detail and observing the rules can become so extreme that it has a paralyzing effect. As well, Squares' rationality and emotional reserve keep them from quickly establishing contact with a variety of people.

Triangle

This figure symbolizes leadership, and many Triangles feel that this is their destiny. The characteristic that most sets true Triangles apart is their ability to concentrate on their main goal. They are energetic, strong personalities. Triangles, like their "relatives" the Squares, are capable of analyzing situations deeply and quickly. But as opposed to Squares, who are focused on details, Triangles concentrate on what's most important, on the essence of a problem.

A Triangle is a very self-assured person who wants to be right about everything! This need to be right and the need to direct situations, to make decisions not only for oneself, but when possible for others as well, makes the Triangle a personality that is constantly jockeying for position and competing with others. Triangles have a very difficult time admitting their mistakes! You can say that they see what they want to see, don't like to change their decision, are often categorical and don't accept others' objections. Fortunately (both for them and for those around them) Triangles are quick and successful learners, although they'll study only what they think will help them reach their main goal.

Triangles are ambitious. If it's a point of honor for a Square means doing work of the highest possible quality, then a Triangle strives for a high position and high status. To put it another way, the Triangle wants to build a career. Triangles make excellent managers. The Triangle's main negative quality is his strong egocentrism and self-referential point of view. As they climb to the top of the power heap they don't demonstrate particular scrupulousness in regard to observing moral norms. Triangles force everything and everyone to revolve around them... If there were no Triangles, perhaps life would lose its point.

Rectangle

This figure symbolizes the state of change. A person who chooses the rectangle rests in that state only at the present moment. This is a form that can be carried within any of the four other figures at various periods of one's life. These are people who are dissatisfied with the way they are currently leading their lives, and who are therefore ever occupied by the search for a better situation. There can be any of a number of reasons for this "rectangular" state, but what they have in common is that change is significant for the given person.

The Rectangle's main psychological state is one of confusion at any given moment in time, of being wrapped up in his own problems and lacking clarity in relation to himself. The most characteristic traits for a Rectangle are the inconsistency and unpredictability of his actions. As a rule, they have low self-esteem. They strive to improve themselves in some area, search for new ways of working and lifestyles. The swift, sharp and unpredictable changes in Rectangles' behavior usually dismay and worry others, who might even consciously avoid having contact with this person who has no core.

Interaction with others is simply a must for Rectangles, and herein lies another difficulty for them. All the same, you do find positive qualities in Rectangles, too, ones which draw in those around them: curiosity, inquisitiveness, a lively interest in all that goes on, and... boldness! At any given period they are open to new ideas, values, and ways of thinking and living, and they absorb new things with ease. True, the opposite side of the coin is that they are excessively trusting and open. For this reason, Rectangles are easily manipulated. "Rectangularism" is only a stage. It will pass!

Circle

The Circle is the symbol of harmony. A person who confidently chooses it is sincerely interested most of all in good interpersonal relations. For the Circle, people are of the highest value. The Circle is the kindest of all the five figures. More often than not, it's the Circle that serves as the "glue" that brings coworkers together, and the family, too. Circles are the best communicators, precisely because they are the best listeners. They possess great sensitivity and the ability to empathize with others. Circles are excellent at "reading" people and can recognize in a second if someone is being deceptive or pretending to be something they aren't.

Circles "root" for their group and are popular among their coworkers. Even so, as a rule they are weak managers and leaders in the business world. First of all, Circles are oriented more toward people than work. As they try to keep the peace, they sometimes avoid taking a hard line and making unpopular decisions. There's nothing worse for a Circle than to step into the middle of an interpersonal conflict. They try to avoid this at any cost, sometimes to the detriment of their work. Second, Circles in general are not particularly decisive, and often can't present themselves properly. Triangles generally easily move past them on their upward path. But Circles are not too worried about who's holding the power. Circles do exhibit an enviable firmness: when it's a question of morals or miscarriage of justice.

One can say that the Circle is a natural psychologist. But he's often a poor organizer – he's missing the Triangle's and Square's traits.

Zigzag

This figure symbolizes creativity and creation, if only because it is the most unique of the five figures and is the only figure that isn't closed. If you decisively chose the zigzag as your main form, then it's likely that you are a truly creative person and nonconformist. You, just like your close relative, Circle, are characterized by imagery and intuition are, only more so. A Zigzag's thoughts make daring leaps from A to Z, and for this reason many people have a hard time understanding Zigzags.

Zigzag's don't get fixate on details, so they simplify their picture of the world to a certain extent; they compose whole harmonious concepts and images, seeing the beauty in everything. Zigzags usually have a well-developed aesthetic sense.

Unlike Circles, Zigzags are not at all interested in building consensus and attain synthesis not by compromising but, on the contrary, by intensifying the conflict of ideas and building a new concept in which this conflict attains resolution and dissolves. In addition, by using their natural ingenuity, they can be totally caustic as they "open others' eyes."

Zigzags simply can't work in highly structured environments. Firmly delineated responsibilities annoy them. They require independence from others in their work, as well as a high degree of stimulation in the workplace.

When that happens, the Zigzag comes alive and begins to fulfill its function– to generate new ideas.

Zigzags are idealists, which is the source of such traits as lack of practicality and naivete.

The Zigzag is the most excitable of the five figures. They are unrestrained and very expressive, which, together with their eccentricity, often makes it difficult for them to bring their ideas to fruition in life. In addition, they are not strong when it comes to details and are not too persistent when it comes to seeing things through to completion – once the newness fades, they quickly lose interest in an idea.

Afterword

When does one's upbringing come to an end? It comes to an end when one acquires wisdom. One's self-education comes to an end when one finds oneself. Peace, calm and harmony come when your desires fade away. If we become who we are, we become child-like, and that means that the distance between adult and child disappears. When there is no distance, there is acceptance. This means that we no longer try to mold our children into something, but simply accept them for who they are. This is what it means to love those close to us.

As you've already noticed, this books doesn't contain any fundamental pedagogical knowledge. It is only an index of the truths which, it would seem, everyone already knows, but which they've forgotten as they've moved through life. The author's task has been to remind you of them.

In this book I haven't touched upon the topic of childhood fears, or the subject of the sexes. Why do some parents have boys and others girls, while some have both? You can find the answers to these questions yourself through your own observations. As far as children's fears are concerned, psychologists have written numerous books on this subject. However, these fears are, primarily, we ourselves. Children's fears are their natural reaction to the unfamiliar and the unknown. And in part, the child simply needs time to come to the conclusion that the object is not threatening in any way. Adults' fears are much more complex: the fear of living, fear of negative outcomes, of being an unknown, of an unstable life. But this is a topic that deserves to be treated separately and is beyond the scope of the current book.

Childrearing should be an easy and pleasant way for each parent to spend time with his or her child. Then life will be a source of more joy and less disappointment. Everyone on the planet has the desire to raise their children through play and to play while raising them. Since this is not an easy task for fathers, it's apropos to quote Thornton Wilder's words to the effect that no man can become a good father until he learns to understand his own father. And mothers would do well to remember the words of Luule Viilma, one of the wisest women of the last century, who said that a person is capable of not reacting to the whole world's opinion, but is incapable of not reacting to his mother's opinion of him. So, the core of a delightful upbringing lies in less criticism and more understanding. I wish you all love and peace.

I would be happy to receive readers' responses and stories about childrearing. You can write to me at **lifewithloveasitis@gmail.com.**

This book presents the author's views and doesn't claim to present the absolute truth on the topic, since you always come to understand the absolute truth on your own.

A separate BIG THANK YOU to SUSAN DOWNING, without whom this book would not have turned out the way it has.

And to end with, a joke:
"Madame, tell me. When you were filling out this form, why did you write that you didn't have children? You have four of them!"
"Goodness, how can you call those children? They're parasites!"

May this happen only in dumb jokes.

Here are some books I'm preparing for publication:

"The Path Through Unhappiness To Happiness"

"The Metaphysics of Pleasure, *or,* Sweet Quagmires", dedicated to alcoholics, gamblers and others who live life in the fast lane.

"Letters about That, *or* The Total Garbage Heap We Call Life"

TABLE OF CONTENTS

From The Author...4
Honesty...6
Independence...11
Habits...14
Personality...19
Over-Sheltering..23
Spoiling..30
Money..38
Punishment...43
Relationship..53
Adolescent Children...61
Brother and Sisters...70
Authorship in the Child`s Fate...................................76
Choosing a Profession..81
The Incomplete Family...88
Abandoned Children...95
Blind Love..102
A Gender Neutral Upbringing...................................108
Why Are Children Born?..112
Appendix With Games..120
Test..134
Afterword..156

www.ingramcontent.com/pod-product-compliance
Lightning Source LLC
Chambersburg PA
CBHW051802040426
42446CB00007B/470